Swift 3 New Features

A fast-paced guide to get you up and running with Swift 3 and its new features

Keith Elliott

BIRMINGHAM - MUMBAI

Swift 3 New Features

First published: October 2016

Production reference: 1041016

Published by Packt Publishing Ltd.
Livery Place
35 Livery Street
Birmingham
B3 2PB, UK.

ISBN 978-1-78646-963-2

www.packtpub.com

Credits

Author

Keith Elliott

Reviewer

Arthur Ariel Sabintsev

Commissioning Editor

Ashwin Nair

Acquisition Editor

Reshma Raman

Content Development Editor

Divij Kotian

Technical Editor

Gebin George

Copy Editor

Charlotte Carneiro

Project Coordinator

Sheejal Shah

Proofreader

Safis Editing

Indexer

Tejal Daruwale Soni

Graphics

Jason Monteiro

Production Coordinator

Aparna Bhagat

About the Author

Keith Elliott is a multitalented professional with unique business and technology experience spanning telecommunications, real estate investment banking, and capital markets. His work is driven simply by problems that need solutions, whether the problem is as simple as his wife's request for a custom to-do list or as complex as interest rate derivatives and foreign exchange hedging. He graduated with an MBA from Columbia Business School with an emphasis in entrepreneurship and an undergraduate degree from Georgia Institute of Technology with a bachelor's in computer engineering.

Keith's own company, GittieLabs LLC, works with startups to provide technology solutions. His vision is to equip students with the real-life experience necessary to succeed in startup and corporate life. You can find his blog on the GittieLabs LLC website, www.gittie.com.

On nights and weekends, Keith can be found spending time with his family, riding motorcycles with his lovely wife, watching football, and rewatching countless hours of WWDC videos.

I would like to thank my wife Grace, children Jadyn, Avery, Tobias, and Cohen, and his little dog Gideon for inspiring and helping me fulfill my dreams.

About the Reviewer

Arthur Ariel Sabintsev is one of the lead iOS engineers at *The Washington Post*. His mobile engineering career includes working for a U.S. Government-funded digital identity startup (ID.me), a Techstars funded video startup (Shelby.tv), and an award winning mobile development agency (Fueled).

He's also spent the last 3 years teaching Swift and Objective-C for General Assembly and writing over a dozen open source iOS libraries for the general public. Before leaving his PhD program, he was an experimental nuclear physicist who worked underground colliding subatomic and subnuclear particles.

www.PacktPub.com

For support files and downloads related to your book, please visit www.PacktPub.com.

Did you know that Packt offers eBook versions of every book published, with PDF and ePub files available? You can upgrade to the eBook version at www.PacktPub.com and as a print book customer, you are entitled to a discount on the eBook copy. Get in touch with us at service@packtpub.com for more details.

At www.PacktPub.com, you can also read a collection of free technical articles, sign up for a range of free newsletters and receive exclusive discounts and offers on Packt books and eBooks.

https://www.packtpub.com/mapt

Get the most in-demand software skills with Mapt. Mapt gives you full access to all Packt books and video courses, as well as industry-leading tools to help you plan your personal development and advance your career.

Why subscribe?

- Fully searchable across every book published by Packt
- Copy and paste, print, and bookmark content
- On demand and accessible via a web browser

Table of Contents

Preface

With the release of Swift 3, Apple is seeking to increase adoption of Swift. The mission of this book is to very quickly get new and seasoned developers up to speed and productive with Swift 3. We will explore the major features introduced to Foundation and the Standard Library. We will also provide commentary on how to convert existing Swift 2.2 projects to Swift 3 and examine Swift's support for running and developing on Linux.

Objectives and achievements

My objective is to introduce you to new concepts available with the release of Swift 3. Our journey together will hopefully lead you to a greater understanding in the following areas:

- Understanding how the *Grand Renaming* will make your code easier to write and understand by other developers
- Getting comfortable with the tools available to write Swift applications on a Mac or on Linux
- Converting your Swift 2.2 projects to Swift 3
- Making you aware of the syntax changes new to Swift 3

What this book covers

Chapter 1, *What Were They Thinking?*, introduces you to Swift 3. Swift is an important language for Apple and its adoption rate has been amazing so far. We will cover the process for how changes to the language are selected and how the community can contribute. In addition, we will cover Swift.org and Apple's Github page as the repositories for everything that is happening in Swift.

Chapter 2, *Discovering New Territories - Linux at Last!*, discusses that, while Mac development was your only supported option up until recently, Swift 3 supports developing and running Swift applications on a Linux machine. Our goal is get your development environment setup on both a Mac and a Linux machine by the end of this chapter. We will write our first Linux application together.

Chapter 3, *Migrating to Swift 3 to Be More Swifty*, will show how to use the Swift Migrator to upgrade our Swift 2.2 projects. We will use a sample project to walk through using the migrator and outline some useful strategies when migrating a Swift project.

Chapter 4, *Changes to Swift's Core Will Have Asking for More*, will quickly highlight the philosophies for writing good Swift APIs. Afterwards, we will spend the remaining chapter on language improvements for referencing and using Objective-C features in Swift 3 and importing code from Objective-C and C to Swift 3.

Chapter 5, *Function and Operator Changes – New Ways to Get Things Done*, will examine what's changed in function declaration and usage and how those changes translate into better Swift code. We will also explain operator changes and highlight several that have been removed from the language.

Chapter 6, *Extra, Extra Collection and Closure Changes That Rock!*, here we are focusing on collection and closure changes in Swift 3. There are several nice additions that will make working with collections even more fun. We will also explore some of the confusing side effects of creating closures in Swift 2.2 and how those have been fixed in Swift 3.

Chapter 7, *Hold onto Your Chair, Advanced Type Changes are Here!*, We are going to cover a few improvements to the language that you might not use on a regular basis. This chapter focuses on *UnsafePointer* types, *typealiases,* and floating point operations.

Chapter 8, *Oh Goodness! Look What is New in the Foundation Framework*, we will discuss the new Measurements and Units API. We will use several examples to hammer in the concepts so that you will leave this chapter better prepared to handle your measurement challenges in the future.

Chapter 9, *Improving Your Code with Xcode Server and LLDB Debugging*, we will cover Xcode Server's capabilities as a continuous integration server and how automated testing can be included to improve your testing workflow. In the second half, we will describe how to use LLDB for debugging your code on Linux.

Chapter 10, *Exploring Swift on the Server*, shows that Swift running on Linux is a big deal, especially with Linux's popularity for hosting and running servers. Swift 3 opens the possibilities for developers to create server-side applications using the same Swift that they use to create applications on iOS, macOS, tvOS, and watchOS. By the end of this chapter, you will have a running server written completely in Swift on a Linux box.

What you need for this book

This book will guide you through the installation of all the tools that you need to follow the examples. You will need to install Webstorm version 10 to effectively run the code samples present in this book.

Who this book is for

To develop in Swift 3 on a Mac, you will need Xcode 8 and macOS Sierra 10.12. If you would like to take advantage of Swift on Linux, you need access to a Linux machine or virtual machine capable of running Ubuntu 14.04.

Conventions

In this book, you will find a number of text styles that distinguish between different kinds of information. Here are some examples of these styles and an explanation of their meaning.

Code words in text, database table names, folder names, filenames, file extensions, pathnames, dummy URLs, user input, and Twitter handles are shown as follows: "Download the `toolchain` file"

A block of code is set as follows:

```
h5> oneMillion = "one million"
error: repl.swift:11:12: error: cannot assign to value: 'oneMillion' is a
'let' constant
oneMillion = "one million"
~~~~~~~~~~~^
repl.swift:2:1: note: change 'let' to 'var' to make it mutable`
let oneMillion = 1\_000\_000`
^~~~
var
```

Any command-line input or output is written as follows:

```
$ swift
```

New terms and **important words** are shown in bold. Words that you see on the screen, for example, in menus or dialog boxes, appear in the text like this: "Next, you select the **Toolchain** you want to develop against, which will only change the Xcode settings"

Warnings or important notes appear in a box like this.

Tips and tricks appear like this.

Reader feedback

Feedback from our readers is always welcome. Let us know what you think about this book-what you liked or disliked. Reader feedback is important for us as it helps us develop titles that you will really get the most out of. To send us general feedback, simply e-mail feedback@packtpub.com, and mention the book's title in the subject of your message. If there is a topic that you have expertise in and you are interested in either writing or contributing to a book, see our author guide at www.packtpub.com/authors.

Customer support

Now that you are the proud owner of a Packt book, we have a number of things to help you to get the most from your purchase.

Downloading the example code

You can download the example code files for this book from your account at http://www.packtpub.com. If you purchased this book elsewhere, you can visit http://www.packtpub.com/support and register to have the files e-mailed directly to you.

You can download the code files by following these steps:

1. Log in or register to our website using your e-mail address and password.
2. Hover the mouse pointer on the **SUPPORT** tab at the top.
3. Click on **Code Downloads & Errata**.
4. Enter the name of the book in the **Search** box.
5. Select the book for which you're looking to download the code files.
6. Choose from the drop-down menu where you purchased this book from.
7. Click on **Code Download**.

Once the file is downloaded, please make sure that you unzip or extract the folder using the latest version of:

- WinRAR / 7-Zip for Windows
- Zipeg / iZip / UnRarX for Mac
- 7-Zip / PeaZip for Linux

The code bundle for the book is also hosted on GitHub at `https://github.com/PacktPubl ishing/Swift-3-New-Features`. We also have other code bundles from our rich catalog of books and videos available at `https://github.com/PacktPublishing/`. Check them out!

Errata

Although we have taken every care to ensure the accuracy of our content, mistakes do happen. If you find a mistake in one of our books-maybe a mistake in the text or the code-we would be grateful if you could report this to us. By doing so, you can save other readers from frustration and help us improve subsequent versions of this book. If you find any errata, please report them by visiting `http://www.packtpub.com/submit-errata`, selecting your book, clicking on the **Errata Submission Form** link, and entering the details of your errata. Once your errata are verified, your submission will be accepted and the errata will be uploaded to our website or added to any list of existing errata under the Errata section of that title.

To view the previously submitted errata, go to `https://www.packtpub.com/books/conten t/support` and enter the name of the book in the search field. The required information will appear under the **Errata** section.

Piracy

Piracy of copyrighted material on the Internet is an ongoing problem across all media. At Packt, we take the protection of our copyright and licenses very seriously. If you come across any illegal copies of our works in any form on the Internet, please provide us with the location address or website name immediately so that we can pursue a remedy.

Please contact us at copyright@packtpub.com with a link to the suspected pirated material.

We appreciate your help in protecting our authors and our ability to bring you valuable content.

Questions

If you have a problem with any aspect of this book, you can contact us at questions@packtpub.com, and we will do our best to address the problem.

1
What Were They Thinking?

Apple's release of Swift was a smashing hit from the very beginning. The language generated a lot of hype and it delivered. Of course, with the introduction of any new programming language, problems and issues will come along for the ride. Apple has carefully cultivated the young language, and has been steadily improving its base and introducing new features, support, and compatibility with its long mainstay incumbent, **Objective-C**. So, why would Apple open-source the language? What is Apple's objective and what does that tell us about the forthcoming release of Swift 3?

The focus of this chapter is to discuss Apple's goals for Swift 3, to show you where you can find the source of official information about new and current development in the language, and to explain how the community of developers will shape the fate of Swift as a language.

Apple's goals for Swift 3

During the *What's New In Swift* lecture from Apple's **World Wide Developer Conference (WWDC)** 2016, Apple engineers outlined several goals for the upcoming release of Swift 3:

- Develop an open community
- Portability to new platforms
- Get the fundamentals right
- Optimize for awesomeness

If you missed the conference, you can watch a replay of the talk on Apple's developer portal. Here's the link for *What's New In Swift*: `https://develo per.apple.com/videos/play/wwdc216/42`.

I want to briefly touch on a couple of themes here as it will provide a base for the material you will find in the remaining chapters:

- Apple believes that for Swift to grow in adoption it needs a strong community. The path to rapid Swift adoption is to include the voices of the community in its development.
- Swift is a general-purpose language that could and should run on any platform. Imagine running Swift on Linux or on the **Internet of Things** (**IoT**) you create or need to control. Apple believes that the Swift language is so capable that they removed the barriers that tied Swift to running on a Mac, opening endless possibilities for platform portability. Apple wants the community to find ways to get Swift to run on other platforms. Today, the Swift team is supporting a port to Linux. Tomorrow, the Swift team could have official support for a wide range of platforms.
- In order to make the first two themes possible, the Swift team needs to get things right from the beginning with Swift 3. Unfortunately, this means that the new changes in Swift 3 do not work well with previous releases of Swift. The Swift 3 release will fix and remove things that were awkward in Swift 2 (and its predecessors). Swift 3 also re-imagines how it interacts with Cocoa and Objective-C to make the APIs that bridge them feel more *Swifty*.

Swift is a really big deal to Apple and expectations from the language are high. Apple has laid out its roadmap for how it expects to reach its goals. In fact, you can stay current with all things Swift by subscribing to one of the mailing lists found here `https://swift.org/co mmunity/#mailing-lists`. The main method for communicating with the Swift community is via mailing lists. You can find mailing lists that cater to general information as well as lists for day-to-day updates on the language. The Swift mailing lists can be a valuable tool that you should not overlook.

In the next section, we will talk about what the open source community means for you as a Swift developer.

Open source Swift

On December 3 2015, Apple open-sourced Swift (including the language, supporting libraries, debugger, and package manager) under the Apache 2.0 license and launched the `https://swift.org/` website on the same day. `https://swift.org/` is the official site to find resources on the various projects that make up Swift. It's your main source to read announcements on all of the development work on the language, from proposals of new features, to links to development branches of Swift code that you can download and test.

`https://Swift.org/` is a website that you will want to bookmark for future reference. The entire Swift codebase is hosted on GitHub and is available for anyone to access. Take a second to think about that. Anyone can download Swift, play around with a binary, build a project, or look under the hood to see how things actually work. For a company of Apple's size and reputation, releasing Swift, the language that they are betting on to power all of their applications, to the community is amazing and should not be taken lightly. This is huge!

Naturally, Apple didn't just hand the language over and walk away. Instead, Apple set up an internal team to shepherd the development process and to be responsible for the day-to-day project management. The open sourced version of the Swift language is comprised of a group of projects each hosted as a separate repository on GitHub. Today, you can find links to six active projects:

- **Swift compiler**: Command line tool
- **Standard library**: Distributed as part of the core language
- **Core libraries**: Provide a higher level functionality
- **LLDB debugger**: Includes the Swift REPL
- **Swift Package manager**: Building projects and distributing them

Each project has a dedicated section on `https://Swift.org/` that explains the project goals and links on how to use both Swift and contribute as a community member. I encourage you to review `https://Swift.org/` to get a better handle on all things Swift from Apple's perspective. Before we end our section on where to find resources on Swift, I do want to briefly discuss what it means to be a community contributor.

The community structure has been well thought out and it's designed to provide strong leadership from members in the community. This structure will guide the on-going development of the language and will hopefully ensure that as the community expands, many new community contributors will have a voice that is heard and respected. See below for the roles that make up members of the community:

- **Project Lead**: Apple is the project lead and will select others from the community to serve in various technical lead positions
- **Core Team**: This small team of engineers is responsible for strategic direction
- **Code Owner**: This title goes to anyone responsible for a specific area of a Swift project codebase
- **Committer**: This role is given to anyone with commit access to a Swift repository
- **Contributor**: This role is reserved for anyone who contributes to a patch or helps with a code review

You can read more about the individual roles in the community on `https://Swift.org/` under the community section. The Swift community is growing and, not unexpectedly, many developers are curious about how to contribute. With that in mind, let's explore how things get done.

Contributing to Swift

There are a few ways that you can help make the community and Swift better. Surprisingly, it's not just by cranking out code. The community needs support with answering questions on the mailing lists. Your answers could range from helping a newbie get a better grasp on a new concept to, going to the opposite extreme, helping a seasoned developer work through a subtle bug. Either way, contributing your knowledge could be valuable to others and would be very much appreciated!

The next option for contributing to the Swift project is by either reporting or triaging bugs. The Swift team uses Jira for defect tracking and you can submit bugs on the project's Jira instance located at `https://bugs.swift.org`.

The final option you have as a developer is to contribute code. There is a formal process for committing code that we will briefly cover. The Swift project prefers small incremental changes to large commits or long-term disconnected feature branches. The Swift team also encourages, but does not enforce, commit messages that describe in detail what your committed code changes include. Code quality is extremely important and is emphasized through mandatory code reviews and pull requests to ensure at least another set of eyes has reviewed all code changes. Think of it this way; your changes will eventually make it into a production environment and have the potential to affect millions of developers that use the Swift language. Do you really want to take of chance introducing a defect that might affect millions of developers?

Swift evolution process

While Apple and the Swift team each have tons of great ideas on where Swift can go, it's important to remember that they aren't the only ones with ideas. In fact, the Swift team fully realizes this, and in response has created a process for you to submit your big or small ideas to help shape the Swift language.

The Swift evolution process encompasses all things related to taking a raw idea from inception through discussion and dialog and hopefully ending at an accepted proposal that developers can implement for production release. The goal of the process is to have active engagement within the community in order to steer the direction of the language while remaining true to the vision of Swift. In practice, that might translate into adding new features that make the language easier to use or removing features that no longer fit the vision of Swift. You can participate by proposing a new idea, or discussing and reviewing the proposals of other community members.

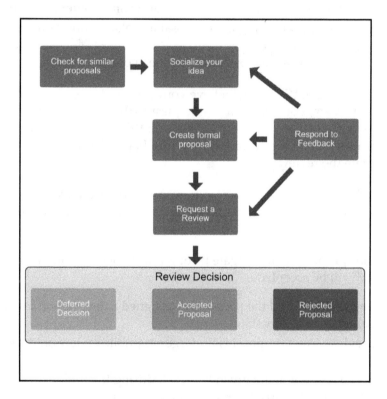

Swift evolution proposal steps

Here are the steps required to get a new idea moved into an accepted proposal:

1. **Check for similar proposals**: It's important to do your homework and make sure that your idea hasn't already been proposed and/or rejected. Spend time reviewing proposals and their states. You can check the Commonly Rejected Proposals list for this task.

2. **Tell others about your idea**: Most of the discussions around new ideas take place on the swift-evolution mailing list. This is where you should create a draft of your idea, along with the problem it addresses and some context on a solution.

3. **Create your proposal**: Using the proposal template found here `https://github.com/apple/swift-evolution/blob/master/-template.md`, you elaborate on your idea and continue to socialize it on the evolution mailing list.

4. **Request a review**: When you believe your proposal is ready for a formal review by the core team, you submit a pull request to the swift-evolution repository `https://github.com/apple/swift-evolution`. When your pull request is accepted, your proposal will be given a proposal number and assigned a core team member to facilitate the review.

5. **Respond to feedback**: It's your job to respond to questions and feedback on your proposal on the mailing list. This is especially important during the review period.

If all goes well, your proposal will navigate through the proposal states below during the review process and will be accepted.

- **Awaiting review**: Until the proposal is assigned a date period for review, your proposal remains in this state.
- **Under review**: Your proposal is undergoing public review on the swift-evolution mailing list.
- **Under revision**: If you are given feedback during the under-review state, you are given an opportunity to address and modify your proposal.
- **Deferred**: Decision postponed because it doesn't meet the criteria for the upcoming major Swift release. In this state, your proposal will be reconsidered when scoping for the next major Swift release.
- **Accepted**: Accepted and new work can begin or is actively being done to implement your accepted proposal. An announcement will also go out to let the community know of a new accepted proposal for the upcoming release.
- **Rejected**: Considered but rejected by the core team.

Here are some key things to remember about the review process. It doesn't start until a core team member (review manager) accepts your pull request for the proposal. Once accepted, the review manager will coordinate a review period with you and any other authors of the proposal to start a formal public review. The review period is a week long in most cases, but can be longer depending on the scope and complexity of changes outlined in the submitted proposal. Finally, the core team, not just the review manager, will make a decision on the proposal using the comments from the swift-evolution mailing list to help base their decision.

Overview of accepted proposals for Swift 3

Each major release of Swift will have high-level goals to which accepted features must adhere. For the Swift 3 release, the Swift team outlined that the primary goal of this release is to solidify and mature the Swift language and development experience.

In their own words, the Swift team went on to stated that While source code breaking changes to the language have been the norm for Swift 1 through 3, we would like the Swift 3.x (and Swift 4+) languages to be as source-compatible with Swift 3.0 as reasonably possible. However, this will still be best-effort: if there is a really good reason to make a breaking change beyond Swift 3, we will consider it and find the least invasive way to roll out that change (for example, by having a long deprecation cycle).

In order to achieve the release goal for Swift 3, each of the following are considered important in terms of getting the basics right for future releases:

- API design guideline
- Automatic application of naming guidelines to imported Objective-C APIs
- Adoption of naming guidelines in key APIs
- Swiftification of imported Objective-C APIs
- Focusing and refining the language
- Improvements to tooling quality

You can learn more about each of these areas on the Swift Evolution repository page as well as see the complete list of implemented proposals, accepted but not yet implemented proposals, and rejected or withdrawn proposals.

Summary

In this chapter we discussed Apple's goals for Swift 3 and the importance of the community's engagement and involvement to the language's development. I also showed you where to find the source of official information about new and current development on the language. Last, we learned how the community can contribute to the development process of Swift as a language. In Chapter 2, *Discovering New Territories – Linux at Last!* We go over developing Swift on Linux.

2
Discovering New Territories – Linux at Last!

Until recently, developing for Swift meant you needed a Mac, loaded with the Xcode IDE. However, all of that changed when Apple open sourced the Swift programming language in December 2015. A brave new world has been opened to us as developers, as Swift can now run on Linux! In addition, you now have access to preview releases and have direct access to the development trunk from which you can download development snapshots (for example, non-official prebuilt binaries of Swift).

This is going to be a packed chapter, and I want to highlight what we will cover. My goal is to show you where to find the latest Swift source for both Mac and Linux. I will also provide instruction on how to use *toolchains* and explain how the Swift package manager works. Last, we will develop our first program on Linux.

Downloading Swift

In order to get started working with Swift 3, you need to download either a prebuilt binary (also known as a *toolchain*) or the source code to build the Swift library yourself. The Swift.org (`https://swift.org`) website hosts a **Download** section `https://swift.org/download/` that maintains a list of releases, previews and snapshots:

- **Release builds**: Maintains links to the current release and older official releases of Swift.
- **Preview builds**: Contains links to developer previews, also known as *seeds* or *betas*. These binaries are not considered final releases but do provide a fairly stable version of the work completed to that date for upcoming releases.
- **Developer snapshots** – Are pre-built binaries from the development branch.

These builds contain the latest development changes and have gone through automated unit testing but are not guaranteed to be stable. Snapshot builds are not put through the full testing process.

 Since learning to build the binary isn't critical to your knowledge of learning Swift 3, we will leave compiling the source as an exercise for you to try on your own at some point. You can find the source code on Apple's GitHub (https://github.com/apple) along with build instructions.

Swift 3 on Mac

To get up and going on a Mac, you simply need to choose the type of Swift *toolchain* you want to develop against. You can choose a version from the **Download** section. Swift on a Mac is included with Xcode, making it really easy to get started. Swift 3 requires you to have macOS 10.11.5 (El Capitan) or later and Xcode 8. Let's walk through the steps together and install Swift 3 on a Mac.

1. **Download a toolchain** – Grab the latest Swift 3 release or preview candidate from the downloads page on https://swift.org/. Xcode is created and maintained by Apple, selecting a release to download from https://swift.org/ will take you to Apple's downloads section on their developer portal.

 An Xcode toolchain is a special binary with a toolchain extension that includes Xcode and all of the tools and libraries that make up Swift (LLVM, LLDB, REPL, and other tools) all targeted at a specific Swift version. You can think of a toolchain as a bundled development environment that you install and extract onto your system to work with a specific release. When you want to try out a different version, you have to download and install the toolchain that corresponds to the target version.

2. **Run the package installer** – This will install Xcode (toolchain).

 The Xcode package that you download for a release or developer snapshot should be digitally signed with a developer ID (Developer ID Installer: Swift Open Source (V9AUD2URP3)) of the open source project to protect against malicious code and tampering. The Swift installer should display a lock on the right side of the title bar. When you click the lock, you should see details on the developer signature.

3. **Select a Toolchain [Optional]** – If this is the only Swift version on your machine, you can skip this step. However, if you have multiple developer snapshots or previews, you can tell Xcode which version to use by navigating to Preferences, choosing **Components** | **Toolchains** or using the **Toolchains** menu listed under **Preferences...** directly:

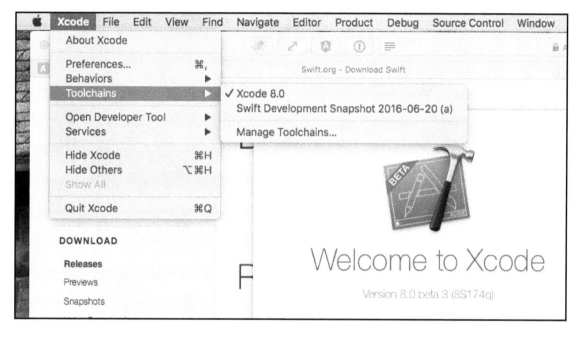

Selecting Toolchains in Xcode 8

4. Next, you select the **Toolchain** you want to develop against, which will only change the Xcode settings. If you want your command line tools settings to change as well, you need to configure those using the *xcrun* and *xcodebuild*.

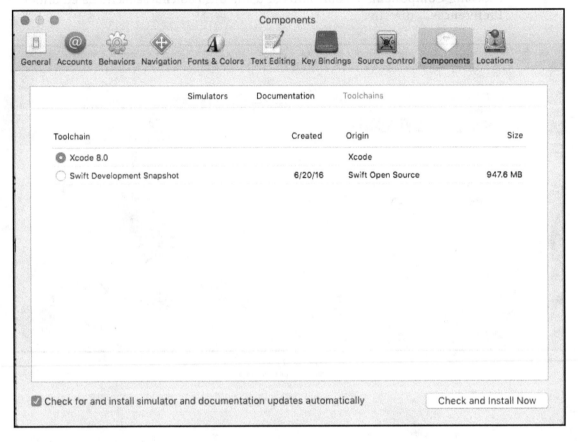

Toolchains menu in Xcode

5. Each command has an option to point to a specified Swift `toolchain`.

```
$ xcrun --toolchain swift
$ xcodebuild --toolchain swift
```

Once you have your *toolchain* installed on your Mac, you simply need to launch Xcode and you can begin developing. Since we will spend the majority of the next few chapters tackling new Swift features using Xcode, we are going to shift gears and spend the rest of this chapter discussing Swift on Linux.

Swift 3 on Linux

The Swift team currently supports installing Linux on Ubuntu 14.04 or 15.10 (64-bit). On Linux, Swift packages are distributed as tar archives. Each package includes the Swift compiler, the LLDB debugger, and tools related to doing development in Swift.

If you don't have access to a Linux box, you can create a virtual machine using VirtualBox `https://www.virtualbox.org` and Vagrant `https://www.vagrantup.com`.

VirtualBox is a virtualization application that runs on multiple platforms and allows you to install another OS. You can download the latest version from `https://www.virtualbox.org/wiki/Downloads`.

Vagrant is a configuration and provisioning package that allows you to install and configure a complete development environment. You can find instructions on how to install and configure a Linux box at this location `https://www.vagrantup.com/`

1. We need to install our required dependencies. Run the following command:

    ```
    $ sudo apt-get install clang libicu-dev
    ```

    - `clang` : The C language front-end for LLVM compiler.
    - `libicu-dev` : An Ubuntu package written in C++ and C that provides a solid full-featured Unicode and local support.

2. We need to download a *toolchain* along with a *.sig* file that serves as the *toolchain*'s digital signature. The *toolchain* has the format `swift-<VERSION>-<PLATFORM>.tar.gz`, and the digital signature file has the same format with extension `.sig`.

3. We are going to install a preview *toolchain* for Ubuntu 14.04. Copy the link for the *toolchain* and download the files to your Linux machine.

4. Download the `toolchain` file:

    ```
    $ wget https://swift.org/builds/swift-3.0-preview-2/ubuntu1404/
    swift-3.0-PREVIEW-2/swift-3.0-PREVIEW-2-ubuntu14.04.tar.gz
    ```

5. Download the digital signature file:

```
$ wget https://swift.org/builds/swift-3.0-preview-2/ubuntu1404
/swift-3.0- PREVIEW-2/swift-3.0-PREVIEW-2-ubuntu14.04.tar.gz.sig
```

6. Import PGP keys for verifying the integrity of our *toolchain*. You only need to download the keys once:

```
$ wget -q -O - https://swift.org/keys/all-keys.asc | gpg --import -
```

7. We verify our downloaded *toolchain* using the PGP key we imported.

8. Refresh your keys and download any newly available certificates:

```
$ gpg --keyserver hkp://pool.sks-keyservers.net --refresh-keys Swift
```

9. Then we verify that the signature file we downloaded is good:

```
$gpg--verify swift-3.0-PREVIEW-2-ubuntu14.04.tar.gz.sig
gpg: Signature made Thu 07 Jul 2016 11:12:12 PM UTC using
RSA key ID 91D306C6
gpg: Good signature from "Swift 3.x Release Signing Key <swift-
infrastructure@swift.org>"
gpg: WARNING: This key is not certified with a trusted signature!
gpg: There is no indication that the signature belongs to the owner.
Primary key fingerprint: A3BA FD35 56A5 9079 C068 94BD 63BC
1CFE 91D3 06C6
```

 If our *gpg* verify statement returns a `Bad signature` then do not open the *toolchain* and report the problem to `swift-infrastructure@swift.org`.

10. Extract the *toolchain* from the archive:

```
$ tar xzf swift-3.0-PREVIEW-2-ubuntu14.04.tar.gz
```

11. We need to include the */usr* directory to our path so that we can execute the swift command for using the REPL environment. Add the Swift *toolchain* to your path:

```
$ export PATH=/home/vagrant/swift-3.0-PREVIEW-2-
ubuntu14.04/usr/bin:"${PATH}"
```

Using the REPL

Once we have Swift installed, we can use the Swift REPL (Read Evaluate Print Loop) environment and give Swift a test run on Linux. The Swift REPL environment and LLDB debugger are tightly linked to the *toolchain*, which aids in Swift type inference, syntax, and expression evaluation. Basically, it makes the compiler, debugger, and REPL environment's jobs easier if there is only one version of Swift to worry about at a time. Let's start the REPL environment and execute a few commands to get familiar with the REPL environment's capabilities.

To start the Swift REPL, you type the swift command:

```
$ swift
```

As we add statements, the REPL environment is smart enough to only execute once you have completely entered a statement. We can create assignment statements, functions, or even entire classes.

At the REPL prompt, let's assign:

```
1> let oneMillion = 1_000_000
oneMillion: Int = 1000000
2> let twoMillion: Int = 2_000_000
twoMillion: Int = 2000000
3> oneMillion + twoMillion
$R0: Int = 3000000
4> $R0 / 1_000_000
$R1: Int = 3
```

Each time we execute a statement, the REPL environment adds the result of the statement on the following line. In our case, we have assigned the numerical values to two different variables (oneMillion and twoMillion). Our third statement adds the two variables together. Notice that the result displays as $R0 Int = 3000000. The Swift REPL environment will create a variable name for you if you don't assign an expression to a variable. We can use the assigned variable in future expressions. In our fourth expression, we use the value stored in $R0to create a new expression that divides the value by 1,000,000.

As I mentioned earlier in this section, the debugger is tightly coupled to the REPL environment. If we add a bad expression, the REPL environment displays the error message as a result:

```
5> oneMillion = "one million"
error: repl.swift:11:12: error: cannot assign to value: 'oneMillion' is a
'let' constant
oneMillion = "one million"
~~~~~~~~~~~^
repl.swift:2:1: note: change 'let' to 'var' to make it mutable`
let oneMillion = 1\_000\_000`
^~~~
var
```

The REPL environment also supports multi-line statements, which you could use to create a function or class. To create a multi-line statement, you simply need to arrow down instead of pressing enter.

If you haven't used the REPL environment in past versions of Swift, you should give it a try. I believe the REPL environment could be very useful for experimenting on creating algorithms or testing out a function for rapid development.

Swift Package Manager

The Swift Package Manager is the Swift Army Knife that allows you to manage your code dependencies, share your own packages, and use the libraries created by others. It's an extremely important tool, one that you need to know in order to do anything productive with Swift. My goal is to provide you with a quick overview and then dive into some examples so we can use it in an example to solidify the core concepts.

Like other languages, Swift allows you to organize and group your Swift code. Swift refers to these groupings as modules. Modules in Swift allow the developer to enforce control on the functionality that is exposed publicly (outside of the module) and the functionality that is only visible within the module.

As developers, we use modules that we create or that other developers create to write our software. When we use other developers' modules, we create a dependency on their code. Swift allows us to create a package, which consists of the Swift code we write plus a manifest file to manage everything we need to build our products. The manifest file that we include in the package defines what we are building, as it includes a package name and a listing of the contents included. A Swift package can have one or more targets, each of which specifies a product or one or more dependencies.

If you have ever worked with Node.js, you can quickly see the similarities between node's package manager and Swift's package manager. Both allow the developer to define manifest files that describe the types of dependencies required to make an application work. Swift's package manager requires you to provide either a relative or absolute URL to the source and the version required. Once provided, the package manager takes over, downloading and compiling the required dependencies for you. In fact, the package manager recursively checks each dependency, evaluating a dependency to see if it has any dependencies and repeats this process until it covers the entire graph. This could be a big task depending on the size of your package.

More Resources:
You can access the source for the Swift Package Manager here: `https://g ithub.com/apple/swift-package-manager`.
You can learn more about how to structure your manifest files here: `https://github.com/apple/swift-package-manager/blob/master/Docum entation/Package.swift.md`
You can get insights on creating your own packages here: `https://githu b.com/apple/swift-package-manager/blob/master/Documentation/De velopingPackages.md`

Our first Swift program

Let's create our first program on Linux using Swift. Our first project will be a package. Create a directory named `guesswho` and then enter the directory:

```
$ mkdir guesswho
$ cd guess who
```

Next we need to initialize a new package with the type being an executable:

```
$ swift package init --type executable
Creating executable package: guesswho
Creating Package.swift
Creating .gitignore
Creating Sources/
Creating Sources/main.swift
Creating Tests/
```

I want to point out a couple of things about the output of swift package init. First, using the swift package init command is optional and meant only to be a utility mechanism for generating files and directories you may need. Second, the package manager expects you to put your sources files within the Sources directory. You can further nest additional directories under the `Sources` directory and the package manager will treat those directories as modules. Finally, when you want to create an executable, you need to include a `main.swift` file in the module's subdirectory or directly within the `Sources` directory in cases when you only have one target. Let's look at an example of a Swift package.

Creating a package with multiple modules:

- `mymodule/Sources/worker/workerbot.swift`
- `mymodule/Sources/manager/manager.swift`

Running swift build on the package above creates:

- `mymodule/.build/debug/workerbot.a`
- `mymodule/.build/debug/manager.a`

Creating a package with one executable and one library module:

- `mymodule/Sources/worker/main.swift`
- `mymodule/Sources/manager/manager.swift`

Running swift build in this time would result in:

- `mymodule/.build/debug/workerbot`
- `mymodule/.build/debug/manager.a`

Notice that our executable doesn't have an extension; however, our library file is created with a `.a` extension.

Open main.swift and remove the code that is currently in there. We are going to replace the existing code with some new logic.

Let's add a function that will recursively call itself and remove the first letter of its input string from the remaining characters, repeating the task until there are no letters left in the string. Once we are finished, we execute a closure to let the caller know we are done:

```swift
func breakWord(combine result:String, input:String, done:(String?)->Void){
    let characterArray = input.characters
    let breakoutCharacter = characterArray.first
    let remainingCharacters = characterArray.dropFirst()
```

```
    if characterArray.count > 0{
        let line = "\n\(breakoutCharacter!):
\(String(remainingCharacters)) "

        let newResult = "\(result) \(line)"
        breakWord(combine: newResult, input:
String(remainingCharacters),
            done: done)
        return
    }
    done(result)
}
```

Next we need to handle the arguments passed when executing our swift program. First in line 1, we store the argument lists as an array. Next, in line 2 we check to make sure we have at least one argument that we can process using our breakWord(combine:) function. Lines 3-8 iterate over our argument list and call our breakWord(combine:) function for each argument. In line 4, we use a closure expression to print the final result of our breakWord(combine:) routine:

```
let arguments = Process.arguments
if arguments.count > 1{
  for n in 1..<arguments.count{
      breakWord(combine: "", input: arguments[n]){ (result) in
          print(result!)
      }
  }
}
else{
    print("no arguments passed")
}
```

If you prefer to see the source all in one place, you can download the code from this chapter using the following link.

Close and save `main.swift` and then compile the program using swift build. You can execute the program by typing `guesswho` along with one or more arguments:

```
$ .build/debug/guesswho Swift 3 New Features
S: wift
w: ift
i: ft
f: t
t:

3:

N: ew
e: w
w:

F: eatures
e: atures
a: tures
t: ures
u: res
r: es
e: s
s:
```

Summary

In this chapter, we covered how to get your development environment configured for Swift development on a Mac or Linux machine. We learned about *toolchains*, using the REPL environment, and the Swift Package Manager. We also created our first Swift package, which we're able to execute on Linux. If you're still with me, we will cover even more awesome things in Swift in the forthcoming chapters! If you're observant, you've probably noticed that our example package lacked a few things. Rest assured, we will take a deep dive into creating and executing tests and debugging techniques in Chapter 9, *Improving Your Code with Xcode Server and LLDB Debugging*. We'll also come back to Linux to tackle a more complicated use case that includes adding dependencies to our package in Chapter 10, *Exploring Swift on the Server*.

Migrating to Swift 3 to Be More Swifty

3

If you're a Swift developer like me, you probably have existing code in Swift 2.2 that you aren't ready to let go of just yet. Thankfully, Xcode 8 and the built in *Swift Migrator* will help you convert your Swift 2.2 projects to Swift 3. We will use a sample project to walk through using the Migrator. We will also go over some useful strategies you can employ when the Migrator fails to convert all of your code properly.

How can you migrate your project…

When you open a Swift 2.2 project in Xcode 8 for the first time, you are given the option to migrate your project to either Swift 2.3 or Swift 3 in order to take advantage of the new SDKs. However, if for some you decide that now is not the right time to convert, you can always do so later. The Swift Migrator tool is accessible in Xcode 8 under the **Edit | Convert | To Current Swift Syntax…** menu.

You will need to convert your code if you want to use the new SDK's available for iOS 10, macOS 10.12, watchOS 3, or tvOS 10. You have two options for migrating your project listed below:

Option1 - Migrating to Swift 3

If you want to build against the latest Swift and use all of the new features of Xcode 8, then choose the migrate to Swift 3 option. The Migrator will modify your source files to adhere to the new Swift 3 syntax.

Option 2 - Migrating to Swift 2.3

If you just want to use the new SDKs and aren't ready or able to migrate to the latest version of Swift, then choose the Swift 2.3 option. Swift 2.3 is Swift 2.2 plus new SDKs. In this migration scenario, the Migrator will modify build settings to use Legacy Swift (Swift 2.2) while making selective source changes to allow your project to build against the new SDKs.

Planning ahead

Let's face it, Xcode is asking you to bravely use its black box tool to make irreversible changes to your project. While I'm a huge Apple fan, I doubt I would ever just press the shiny new migrate button without thinking about what could go wrong in the process. I'm not in the business of scrapping projects and starting from scratch. Honestly, who really is? To avoid a potentially terrible time with the Migrator, you really should consider doing everything listed below as pre-work before migrating your project:

1. Ensure that your existing codebase is making use of a version control system such as Git (`https://git-scm.com`) or Subversion (`https://subversion.apache.org`). If you run the Migrator and the output doesn't convert things as expected (or other unexpected things happen), you will have peace of mind that you can always get back to your original version.

2. Make sure your project compiles on the latest version of Xcode (7.3 or 7.3.1). You want to make sure everything, including your tests, runs as expected under Xcode 7. If your project does not build and run as a Swift 2.2 project, you are just asking for trouble by using the Migrator at this point. Make sure things work now before migrating to Swift 2.3 or Swift 3. Your goal is to have your tests pass now and after the migration.

3. Make sure that every target you want converted builds with the active scheme. The Swift Migrator uses the active scheme in Xcode to determine which source files it should examine for migration. You can verify the targets that the Migrator will consider by looking at the settings of your scheme using the **Edit Scheme** menu. Once there, switch to the build tab of the scheme and make sure that all targets you want migrated are checked off.

You can add a new scheme to your project and include all of the targets. Using a separate scheme for migration will ensure that you don't modify settings on your main schemes. You can remove the scheme after the migration.

If your project uses Carthage or CocoaPods, or another projects that is not built along with your main project, then you have two options:

- **Integrate the outside projects into your main project:** Using this option means that you intend to copy the source files of the other projects into your existing project. I would be hesitant in doing this unless you really have a good handle on how the project is structured and intend to maintain it going forward. Once you copy the files in, you will be disconnected from updates and continued work happening in the project. Updating in the future would require you to perform the same copy, paste, and configure drill each time.

- **Do nothing, meaning you won't convert at this time:** With this option, you migrate just your code and continue to link to any 3rd party project without migrating. This could be a pretty good option to consider as the owner of the outside project might have better insights on how to migrate the project but just has not done so yet. If it's not your project, you might be better off waiting for an update from the owner and maintainers of the project. Chances are good that you can continue to use the 3rd party project as is. A last trend that developers are implementing is to create Swift 2.3 and Swift 3 branches to ease later transitions while developing with Xcode 8 betas.

Migrating with Xcode's Swift migration tool

Once you've done your pre-work, it's time to migrate your code. For our purposes, we are going to use a simple Tic Tac Toe project that you can download from the Packt website:

1. **Launch Xcode 8 and open the Tic Tac Toe project**: On first launch, Xcode will ask you if you want to migrate your Swift 2.2 project to use the latest SDKs. Choose Convert to start the migration.

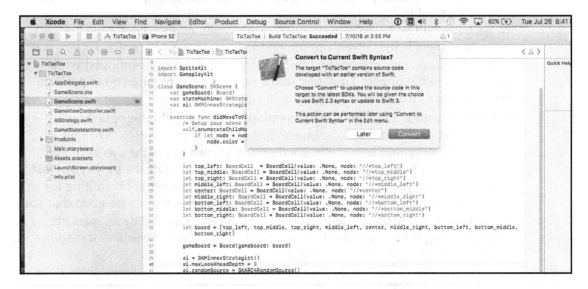

2. **Choose either Swift 2.3 or Swift 3**: After choosing to convert, you will be prompted with another screen that basically lets you know that Xcode is going to modify your files. You are also told that, once the migration is over, you will be given the option to accept the changes or dismiss them without permanently changing your project's files. The modal dialog also gives you a disclaimer that the Swift Migrator isn't perfect and you might have to make additional changes once the migration has completed. Press **Next** and then choose Swift 3.

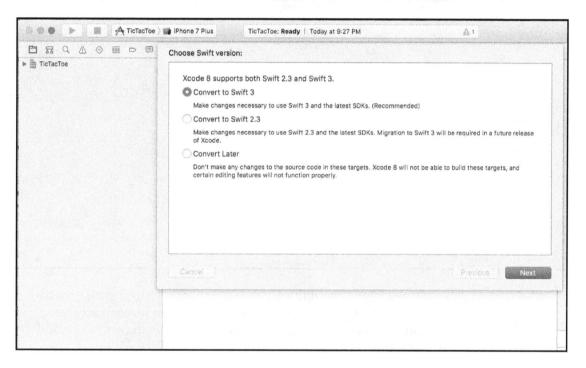

3. **Choose the targets to convert**: If you have a project with multiple targets, you need to make sure that you have selected a scheme that will build all the targets you want migrated to the newest Swift (or Swift 2.3). In our case, there is only one target to convert and it should already be checked off. Should you want to skip a target, you just need to uncheck its corresponding checkbox.

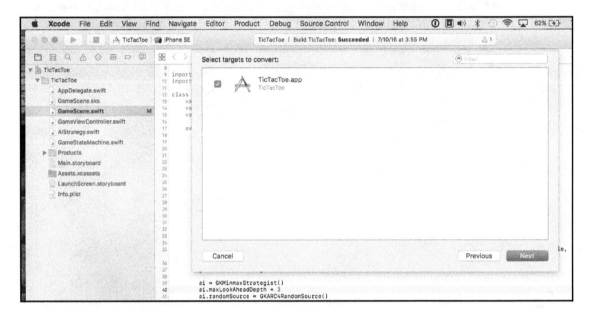

You can run the migration multiple times on a project. If you prefer not to modify your schemes, you could just run the migration for each scheme that you want converted. Just make the selected scheme the active one and start the migration.

4. **Review changes on the preview screen:** After selecting the targets and pressing **Next**, the Migrator tool will begin its work. Once the process is finished, you are prompted with a preview screen containing before and after changes for you to review. Every source file that Xcode modified will be available in the preview window. It is highly recommended that you examine each of the files to make sure you understand the code changes and agree with the recommended changes before accepting them.

5. When reviewing changes, you have options on what you want permanently modified. Each modified file has a numbered listing of changes that you can discard or further modify. You discard a particular change in a file by expanding the button on an individual highlighted change and selecting the dismiss action. At the file level, you can discard changes to a file by unchecking the file on the left sidebar view.

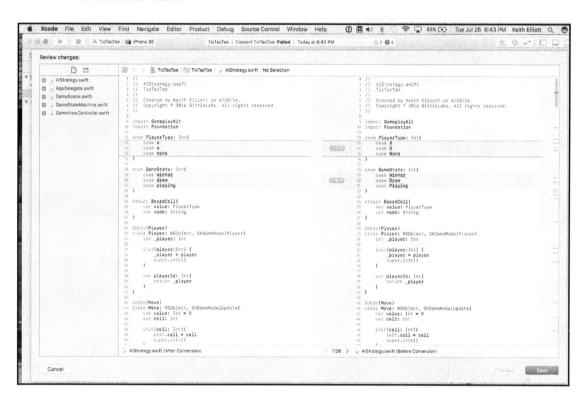

6. **Save your changes:** Once you are finished reviewing changes, press the **Save** button. You will be prompted with a confirmation dialog warning you that the changes will be final. You won't be able to revert using the migration tool once you give the Swift Migrator approval to apply all of the changes. Click the **Continue** button to confirm that you do want to accept the changes.

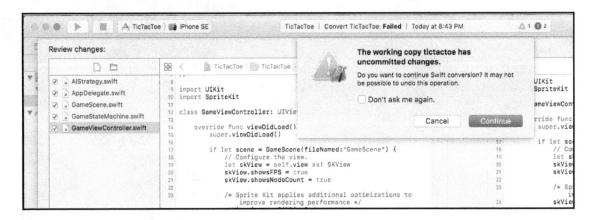

Once you save the changes, the migration is complete. Xcode will try to compile your project and will let you know if there are any build issues. In our case, we have a warning and two build errors. The warning is telling us that we are not using all of the recommended project settings. Go ahead and double-click the warning to have Xcode change our project settings to the recommended ones. In this case, Xcode is recommending that we use Whole Module Optimization.

Whole Module Optimization is a build setting that lets the compiler consider the entire module when making advanced optimizations of your code. When the compiler has module-wide visibility of your code, optimization decisions are made with more information about how an affected routine is used throughout the module and not just within a single file. Better optimizations result in faster code. You can learn more about Whole Module Optimization and options for optimizing Swift performance by viewing the Optimizing Swift Performance lecture given at WWDC 2015 https://developer.apple.com/videos/play/wwdc215/49/.

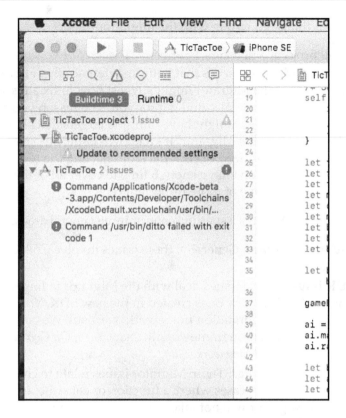

The remaining build errors may or may not show up on your machine. In my case the errors are due to the fact that I had previously built the project using Xcode 7.3.1. Each time you build a project, Xcode caches the intermediate products from a compilation to improve future builds. If part of your code hasn't changed, Xcode uses the cached byproducts to streamline recompilation. This cached data is stored in a folder that Xcode uses for future builds. In my case the derived data folder contained code that was no longer relevant for the project given the project's migration to Swift 3 and Xcode 8.0. Clean your project with the Product > Clean command. Your project should now compile successfully.

Troubleshooting when things go wrong with the migration

Unfortunately, not all projects will convert perfectly. The `https://swift.org` website maintains a list of known Migrator issues that you can reference (`https://swift.org/migration-guide/`). For example, the Migrator might suggest how to fix an issue via a fixit in the editor margin without automatically doing it for you. The reason you might see a fixit in this example is because your project might have multiple targets that share some form of dependence, which can confuse the Migrator. It's a known issue, but an easy one to deal with after the migration. You just need to click the fixit selecting the recommended action, and Xcode will do the rest. We don't have enough time to cover all of the known issues with migrations, but we will cover some of more important ones.

We can categorize known Migrator issues into one of three general areas:

1. **Standard library issues**: Generally, these issues involve Collection routines and types
2. **New SDK issues**: These issues deal with the Migrator failing to correlate old types and protocols to new ones created in the new SDK. You might also run into issues related to the Foundation framework overhaul. We cover the major changes to the Foundation framework in `Chapter 8`, *Oh Goodness! Look What is New in the Foundation Framework*.
3. **Swift 3 language changes**: These Migrator issues relate to changes to the language for Swift 3. In cases where a function or construct is no longer available in Swift 3, the Migrator will not take any action and you will need to manually change the code.

You will need to use a combination of the warning/error messages generated along with the known issues page listed on the `https://swift.org` website to determine how to fix build errors that surface after a migration. If a fixit hint is not provided in the editor margin, you will have to manually correct the issue.

Quick strategies for addressing issues

1. **Fixit suggestions**: After the migration finishes, examine the warnings/errors section for fixit actions. Each of these will give you a recommendation on how to fix the code in question. Simply choose the actions and Xcode will apply the code change.

2. **Migrator comments**: Even when your project compiles, there is still a possibility that the Migrator missed something during the conversion that could not be handled. In these cases, the Migrator leaves /*Migrator FIXME: ...*/ comments in your code. You'll want to search for these and decide if you need to manually make a change once you have evaluated the code block.

3. **Use the new Foundation framework value types**: When inspecting your project code, you might see that Swift is casting types to "NS" prefixed types. You probably don't want legacy Foundation types when using Swift 3. Again, the Migrator does a pretty good job of finding and correcting these; however, you are still advised to do a manual search for the "NS" prefix. If you find any 'NS' prefix occurrences, you will have the opportunity to determine if each is correct or if you should use a new Foundation type without the "NS" prefix. In Chapter 8, *Oh Goodness! Look What is New in the Foundation Framework*, we will cover Foundation changes, including the new value types.

4. **User-defined collection types might generate migration issues**: In Swift 3, collections need to handle moving forward and backward through their collection of items. You will need to adopt the new Collection protocol (https://developer.apple.com/reference/swift/collection) functions that define how you increment the index. If your collection supports decrementing, there is a new protocol function for that as well. Last, there is a protocol function that allows your collection to support randomly accessing an item. If you see errors associated with your custom collections not adhering to the Collection protocol, it's likely that you have not added one or more of the new protocol functions below:

   - func index(after: Index) -> Index
   - func index(before: Index) -> Index
   - func index(_: Index, offsetBy: Int) -> Index
   - func distance(from: Index, to: Index) -> IndexDistance

5. **Removed features in Swift 3**: An example of this would be the C-style for-loop, which has been removed from Swift 3. You will have to manually re-write it as a for...in statement.

Hopefully, at this point, you are getting the idea that the Migrator is going to handle most of your everyday use cases. For those issues, you will need to use the warning and error messages to decipher what's going on. The first place to check should be the known issues section on Swift.org.

Summary

The Swift Migrator is a great tool that saves you time when you need to migrate Swift 2.2 projects to Swift 3 (or Swift 2.3). We learned that we have to migrate our existing Swift 2.2 projects to Swift 3 to take advantage of everything Xcode 8 has to offer. We also learned that we can use the new SDKs without migrating to Swift 3 by choosing to migrate to Swift 2.3 (Swift 2.2 plus new SDKs). At any point in the future, we can use the **Edit | Convert | To Current Swift Syntax...** menu to launch the migration tool. Finally, we learned that the Migrator isn't perfect and that it might not convert everything. We might have to make some manual changes to get things to work after the migration has finished. In the next chapter, we will begin covering Swift 3's core language changes.

4

Changes to Swifts Core Will Have You Asking for More

Many of the libraries have been touched to pull off this effort including-the Swift standard library, all of Cocoa and Cocoa Touch frameworks, Core Graphics, and Grand Central Dispatch. With the release of Swift 3, we can expect changes that reduce the awkwardness of the language's link to Objective-C, exuding way more *Swifty-ness*. The Swift team has introduced new API guidelines with the intention of giving the language its own character. The result is a huge renaming and refactoring effort that flows throughout the language. Swift 3 has undergone a huge facelift in terms of its interaction with Objective-C and C APIs. The Swift team is aiming to make your development experience feel more like Swift and less like directly dumping Objective-C into your code. Swift is its own language and should have its own feel just like any other programming language. Yet prior versions of Swift were heavily influenced by the need to interact with Objective-C and C APIs.

In this chapter, we will quickly highlight the philosophies for writing good Swift APIs. Afterward, we will spend the remaining chapter on language improvements for referencing and using Objective-C features in Swift 3 and importing code from Objective-C and C to Swift 3. Every language change to Swift 3 is covered by one or more Swift Evolution proposals. As we cover a new feature, I'll also provide the proposal number that documents the rationale behind the change. While knowing the actual rational for a new feature is not critical to your understanding of how to implement its code, I think it is interesting to know the efforts and sometimes debates behind why a particular change was implemented. The Swift Evolution repository contains tons of information on accepted and rejected proposals. If you are a careful observer, you will also see proposals that were accepted for the Swift 3 release but didn't get implemented in time for the release.

The grand renaming

Let's start with the proposals for the Swift API Design Guidelines. The Grand Renaming proposals represent, collectively, a very large undertaking and are covered by proposals *SE-0005, SE-0006, SE-0086,* and *SE-0088*. Implementing the API guidelines represents the largest change to the language for Swift 3. I couldn't possibly cover every API change resulting in the Grand Renaming proposals in this short book. Thankfully, you don't have to understand every line that changed in the libraries to be productive with Swift 3. You have two fantastic resources that will pay dividends with very little effort on your part. The first resource is the Swift migration tool which converts existing Swift projects to the latest syntax. When you use the Swift migrator, you can convert your Swift 2.2 projects to Swift 3 and receive most of the changes for free. The second extremely valuable resource is the Swift API Guidelines, which were developed to help make your code more *Swifty*. The Swift API Guidelines are based on the following principles as quoted on `https://swift.or g/documentation/api-design-guidelines/`:

- **Clarity at the point of use**: This is your most important goal. Entities such as methods and properties are declared only once but used repeatedly. Design APIs to make those uses clear and concise. When evaluating a design, reading a declaration is seldom sufficient, always examine a use case to make sure it looks clear in context.
- **Clarity is more important than brevity**: Although Swift code can be compact, it is a *non-goal* to enable the smallest possible code with the fewest characters. Brevity in Swift code, where it occurs, is a side-effect of the strong type system and features that naturally reduce the boilerplate.
- **Write a documentation comment**: This for and every declaration. Insights gained by writing documentation can have a profound impact on your design, so don't put it off.

For more details on adopting these guidelines, please refer to the WWDC 2016 lecture on Swift API Guidelines at `https://developer.apple.com/videos/play/wwdc2016/403/`.

Referencing Objective-C code in Swift 3

With Swift 3, we get a slew of changes that make working with Objective-C and C APIs more enjoyable. We are going to cover the important changes that will make writing code more productive in Swift 3.

Referencing the Objective-C selector of property getters and setters - SE-0064

In Objective-C, we can use a type called a **selector** to reference the name of a method. Swift 2.2 introduced `#selector` expressions to remove the error-prone nature of providing string literals as the selector name. In Swift 3, the language builds on #selector expressions by allowing you to reference getter and setter methods. This feature allows us to refer to getter and setter properties of objects. Let's look at an example to see how we could access the setter for one of the properties on our `ClassRoom` class:

```
class ClassRoom: NSObject{
    var roomNum: String
    init(roomNum: String){
        self.roomNum = roomNum
    }
}

let classRoom = ClassRoom(roomNum: "1-D1")
classRoom.perform(#selector(setter: ClassRoom.roomNum), with: "2-D3")
```

We can now access the setter for the `roomNum` using `#selector(setter: ClassRoom.roomNum)` or the getter using `#selector(getter: ClassRoom.roomNum)`. Once we have our reference, we can use any of the NSObject perform methods available in Objective-C.

 You can read the proposal at `https://github.com/apple/swift-evolution/blob/master/proposals/64-property-selectors.md`

Referencing Objective-C key paths [SE-0062]

Similar to selectors, using Objective-C *keypaths* in Swift 2.2 required us to use string literals. Swift 3 introduces the `#keyPath` expressions to improve accuracy by replacing error-prone string literals with objects that can be checked at compile time. Our example below demonstrates how keypaths were done in Swift 2.2 and how referencing keypaths improves with Swift 3.

For Objective-C:

```
class Employee: NSObject{
    var firstName: String
    var lastName: String
    var boss: Employee?
    init(firstName: String, lastName: String, boss: Employee? = nil){
        self.firstName = firstName
        self.lastName = lastName
        self.boss = boss
    }
}

let bossMan = Employee(firstName: "Jack", lastName: "Spark")
let rocko = Employee(firstName: "Rocky", lastName: "Jones", boss: bossMan)
```

For Swift 2.2:

```
rocko.value(forKeyPath: "Employee.boss.firstName")
```

For Swift 3:

```
#keyPath(Employee.boss) // => boss
rocko.value(forKeyPath: #keyPath(Employee.boss.firstName)) // => Jack
```

In our Swift 3 example above, we use the #keyPath expressions that are compile time checked that allow us to safely access values.

 You can read the proposal at https://github.com/apple/swift-evolution/blob/master/proposals/0 062-objc-keypaths.md

Importing code from Objective-C and C APIs to Swift 3

If you maintain Objective-C or C libraries and want to expose cleaner syntax for Swift, this section is for you! We now have the ability to provide more control over how constants, global functions, and generics are imported from Objective-C and C into Swift.

Importing Objective-C constants as Swift types [SE-0033]

Constants with global scope, defined in header files, are imported with the same global scope in Swift. In many cases, it would be more helpful to have related constants grouped together. In Swift 3, you can now annotate your type declarations with NS_STRING_ENUM or NS_EXTENSIBLE_STRING_ENUM to have those declarations imported as members of a common type.

Importing as Struct

If you want your constants to be imported as members of a struct, then add NS_EXTENSIBLE_STRING_ENUM to the end of your constant type declaration. For more consistent importing into Swift, name your constants using the same type as a prefix. In our example, we created a MPPlatformIdentifier type that we use as a prefix to name our constants: MPPlatformIdentifierIOS, MPPlatformIdentifierMacOS.

For Objective-C:

```
typedef NSString * MPPlatformIdentifier NS_EXTENSIBLE_STRING_ENUM;
MPPlatformIdentifier const MPPlatformIdentifierIOS;
MPPlatformIdentifier const MPPlatformIdentifierMacOS;
```

This imports into Swift as:

```
struct MPPlatformIdentifier : RawRepresentable {
    typealias RawValue = String
    init(rawValue: RawValue)
    var rawValue: RawValue { get }
    static var IOS: MPPlatformIdentifier { get }
    static var macOS: MPPlatformIdentifier { get }
}
```

Importing as Enum

Your other option is to have your constants imported as an enumeration type. Your constants are imported as an enum when you add NS_STRING_ENUM to the end of your type. Each constant that you define using this new type will be added to the enum in Swift.

For Objective-C:

```
typedef NSString * MPVersionEnum NS_STRING_ENUM;
MPVersionEnum const MPVersionEnumV1;
MPVersionEnum const MPVersionEnumV2;
MPVersionEnum const MPVersionEnumV3;
```

This imports into Swift as:

```
enum MPVersionEnum: String{
    case V1
    case V2
    case V3
}
```

 You can read the proposal at `https://github.com/apple/swift-evolut ion/blob/master/proposals/33-import-objc-constants.md`

Importing Objective-C lightweight generics [SE-0057]

In Swift 2, you could import and interact with Objective-C lightweight generics. While you could import lightweight generics of any form into Swift 2, only the Foundation types (`NSArray`, `NSSet`, and `NSDictionary`) preserved their type information after import.

 You can learn more about lightweight generics by reading the Swift documentation on the subject here: `https://developer.apple.com/library/content/documentation/Swif t/Conceptual/BuildingCocoaApps/InteractingWithObjective-CAPIs. html`

With Swift 3, you can import your own Objective-C generics without losing information on the type. In our example below, we have several property types defined using Foundation collection types and a custom generic class. Notice that in both Swift 2 and Swift 3, generics import their type information correctly for the Foundation collection types.

For Objective-C:

```
@property NSArray<MyClass *> * myClasses;
@property NSDictionary<NSString *, MyClass *> * myClassDictionary;
@property NSSet<MyClass *> *mySet;
@property MyCollection<MyClass *> *myCollection;

@interface MyCollection<__covariant ObjectType> : NSObject
  -(void) addItem:(ObjectType)item;
@end
```

Imports into Swift 2 as:

```
var myClasses: [MyClass]
var myClassDictionary:  [String : MyClass]
var mySet: Set<MyClass>
var myCollection: MyCollectionMyCollection Classfunc addItem(item:
AnyObject!)
```

Sadly, we lose the type information for our custom generic property `myCollection`, when importing into Swift 2. Swift rightly determines that the `myCollection` property is of `MyCollection` type, but the parameterized data is lost. Since we lost our type information on import, accessing `addItem()` of `myCollection` class results in a method signature that uses `AnyObject` for the parameter type. This is a subpar result as we expect the type to be `MyClass`, matching the Objective-C signature.

In Swift 3, this import issue is fixed. Our custom Objective-C generics are imported as expected. Examining our Swift 3 import, we can see that all of our generics keep their type information and our class methods will completely match their Objective-C counterparts for our custom generic classes.

Imports into Swift 3 as:

```
var myClasses: [MyClass]
var myClassDictionary:  [String : MyClass]
var mySet: Set<MyClass>
var myCollection: MyCollection<MyClass>
MyCollection Class
func addItem(_ item: MyClass)
```

You can read the proposal at :
https://github.com/apple/swift-evolution/blob/master/proposals/0
057-importing-objc-generics.md

Importing as member [SE-0044]

Many C APIs provide functions that allow you to create, access, and modify C structures. Importing these libraries as-is will add these functions to your global namespace in Swift. While this is fine in many cases, it might be preferable to group these imports under common types in Swift. Swift 3 allows us to use the CF_SWIFT_NAME macro to control how initializers, properties, and methods display in Swift. Let's look at how we can accomplish these tasks.

Defining an initializer

We can modify a C function to create a Swift initializer by appending a CF_SWIFT_NAME macro to the function definition in the header file. To tell Swift we want the function added as an initializer on a specific type, we need to provide the type (MyPlatform) followed by a dot and the *init* format we want (that is the parameters from the C function definition). Swift will import our new initializer as an extension on MyPlatform, representing our common type.

 The common type needs to exist for Swift to add any extensions. Swift will not create this type for you and will fail silently if no type exists.

For C:

```
MyPlatform* MyPlatformWithIdentifier(MPPlatformIdentifier identifier)
CF_SWIFT_NAME(MyPlatform.init(identifier:));
```

This imports into Swift as:

```
extension MyPlatform { init(identifier: MPPlatformIdentifier) }
```

Creating getters and setters

In addition to initializers, we can also create computed properties. We can define the getters and setters that will be imported into Swift. For the property's getter, we need to add the CF_SWIFT_NAME macro to the end of the C function that will serve as the getter and provide a common type and a property name. Our setter will be similar in that we add the macro to the C function that serves as our setter property. See below for the syntax in action. In Swift 3, the getter and setter will be added to the common type MyPlatform using an extension.

For C:

```
//getter
MPPlatformIdentifier MyPlatformGetIdentifier(MyPlatform *platform)
CF_SWIFT_NAME(getter:MyPlatform.platformId(self:));

//setter
Void MyPlatformSetIdentifier(MyPlatform *platform, MPPlatformIdentifier
identifier) CF_SWIFT_NAME(setter:MyPlatform.platformId(self:newValue:));
```

This imports into Swift as:

```
extension MyPlatform {
var platformId: MPPlatformIdentifier { get set }
}
```

Adding methods

We can group methods under a common type during our import into Swift 3. This is accomplished using the `CF_SWIFT_NAME` macro appended to the C function definition in our header file. You will need to provide the macro a common type and a method signature that uses the same number of variables as the C function. Swift will handle determining the parameter type. You just need to provide names you want to use as the signature in Swift.

For C:

```
MPPlatformIdentifier MyPlatformRetreiveId(MyPlatform *platform,
MPPlatformIdentifier identifier)
CF_SWIFT_NAME(MyPlatform.retreiveId(self:identifier:));
```

This imports into Swift as:

```
extension MyPlatform {
    func retreiveId(identifier: MPPlatformIdentifier) ->
MPPlatformIdentifier
}
```

Creating static variables

Finally, we can import global variables as static variables associated with a common type in Swift 3. We just need to provide a common type and variable name to our `CF_SWIFT_NAME` macro. Our static variable will be added to the common type in Swift via an extension.

For C:

```
extern const MPPlatformIdentifier *MyPlatformTVOS
CF_SWIFT_NAME(MyPlatform.tvOS);
```

This imports into Swift as:

```
extension MyPlatform { static var tvOS: MPPlatformIdentifier }
```

 You can read the proposal at:
https://github.com/apple/swift-evolution/blob/master/proposals/0
044-import-as-member.md

Summary

We just finished covering the principles of Swift's API Guidelines. In addition, I provided you with resources on how to find the Swift Evolution proposals that document the motivations for each change. We also covered new features to work with `#selector` and `#keyPath` expressions when working with Objective-C APIs in Swift. Finally, we explored working with C APIs and controlling how they are imported into Swift 3. In the next chapter, we will cover more language changes. Stay tuned as we still a have a lot of new things to cover!

5
Function and Operator Changes – New Ways to Get Things Done

If you want to write useful code in Swift, or in any programming language, you have to, at the very least, create functions and use operators. In this chapter, we will examine what's changed in function declaration and usage and how those changes translate into better Swift code. We will also explain operator changes and highlight several that have been removed from the language.

Continuing the theme from the last chapter, I will provide you the Swift Evolution proposal numbers. Let's get started!

Function declaration changes

Swift provides a very flexible set of rules for defining functions. You can create functions with no parameters, with parameters, or even with argument labels. Every Swift function has a type, parameters (or no parameters), and a return type. For Swift 3, the language has been tweaked to make things more consistent and less complex.

Consistent parameter labeling [SE-0046]

Parameter labels are used for naming each argument in the function definition. In Swift 2.2 and earlier, function parameters could be defined with a local and an external label. The local argument label is required as this label is used to refer to the parameter in the body of the function. The external argument label, when provided, was used in the actual function call. You can think of the external label as your *shiny descriptive name at the call site* to provide good insight into what the argument represents. The internal label is, as the name implies, the name your function uses in the implementation of your logic. Since no one sees that local parameter, you could make it shorter to save some keystrokes.

Here's where things get interesting. By default, Swift 2.2 drops your external name when your function is called. Further adding to the confusion, Swift uses your local name as the external name for any remaining parameters, when external names are not present. The truly odd thing is that Swift only does this for functions. When you create a class, structure, or enumeration initializer (a special type of function to set initial values), Swift will create an external name for every parameter.

 Swift Enumerations can be defined using a raw-value type. When you create a Swift enum using a raw-value, you will either get an initialized enum or nil. You can read more about Swift enums at https://developer .apple.com/library/prerelease/content/documentation/Swift/Conc eptual/Swift_Programming_Language/Enumerations.html#//apple_re f/doc/uid/TP41497-CH12-ID145

The main reason for dropping the first argument name seems to be for historical correctness with Objective-C. Objective-C developers were instructed to incorporate the first parameter name into the function name. This same behavior was adopted by Swift and may have been a side effect of the initial translation of Objective-C libraries to Swift via the migrator.

Swift is an evolving language and is getting better with each new version. To stay consistent with the new API naming guidelines, Swift 3 now defaults to using the local names as the external names for all arguments including the first one.

In Swift 2.2:

```
func gettingSwiftyUsingPeopleNamed(names: [String],
                                   descriptionNames: [String],
                                   shouldCapitalize: Bool){
    // our function only has local names so those are the ones used
}

gettingSwiftyUsingPeopleNamed(["Joe", "Mark", "Roy", "Jessica"],
        descriptionNames: ["Awesome", "Silly", "Tall", "Short"],
        shouldCapitalize: true)
```

In Swift 3:

```
func gettingSwiftyUsing(names: [String],
                        descriptions:[String],
                        shouldCapitalize: Bool){
    // our function only has local names so those are the ones used
}

gettingSwiftyUsing(names: ["Joe", "Mark", "Roy", "Jessica"],
descriptions: ["Awesome", "Silly", "Tall", "Short"],
shouldCapitalize: true)
```

 Last thought — if you prefer to not use argument labels in your function calls, you can suppress them using an underscore as the external name. This works for any of the argument positions.

```
func boxit(_ width: Double, _ height: Double){
    // argument label will be omitted in function call
}

boxit(23, 14)
```

 You can read the proposal at the following link https://github.com/app le/swift-evolution/blob/master/proposals/46-first-label.md

Removing currying func syntax in declaration [SE0002]

In Swift 2, you had the ability to create curried functions; which were rather confusing and seem to have little value in Swift. Much of the developer confusion in using them centers on whether the curried arguments are part of the main argument list or if the curried arguments signify the beginning of the argument list for a new function. Let's consider the following example that uses curried arguments:

```
func curried(cosx: Int)(siny: Int) -> Float {
    return (Float(cosx) * Float(siny)) / Float(cosx)
}

let result = curried(2)(siny:3)
```

It's extremely confusing to tell if the `(siny: Int)-> Float` is part of the argument. The Swift team ultimately decided that we just don't need this in the language. Therefore, Swift 3 removes this syntax and suggests that you re-write your function to return a closure instead:

```
func curriedV2(cosx: Int)->(Int)->Float{
    return { siny in
        (Float(cosx) * Float(siny)) / Float(cosx)
    }
}

let intermediateFunctionReturn = curriedV2(2)
let result2 = intermediateFunctionReturn(3)
```

In our revised example, we define our function to return a closure. We then assign the result of this initial call to a variable named `intermediateFunctionReturn`. Last, we call the `intermediateFunctionReturn` closure, passing our Int argument, to get our final result.

 You can read the proposal at `https://github.com/apple/swift-evolut ion/blob/master/proposals/2-remove-currying.md`

Warning on Unused Results by Default [SE-0047]

Attributes are special constructs that you apply to a declaration or type. You specify an attribute using the @ symbol followed by a name and optionally any attribute arguments in parentheses.

```
@<attribute name>
@<attribute name>(attribute arguments)
```

In Swift 2, the `@warn_unused_result` attribute is applied to a function or method to let the compiler know that it should provide a warning to the user if the attributed method or function is called without using the result. The `@warn_unused_result` attribute also allows you to provide either a message or `mutable_variant` attribute argument. The `mutable_variant` option is used when you want to let the developer know the name of the mutating method that accomplishes the same thing. The intent of using the attribute is to give guidance to the developer using your method, that the returned value is important and should be used.

For example, Swift 2 provides a `sort()` method and a `sortInPlace()` method (mutating) on the Foundation collection classes. If you were to call `sort()` (non-mutating) on an array but not use the result, then the compiler would warn you that you might really need the `sortInPlace()` method, which mutates the array and doesn't return anything. You can see an example usage of the `@warn_unused_result` below.

```
@warn_unused_result(mutable_variant="sortInPlace")
        public func sort() -> [Self.Generator.Element]
```

The main issue that developers have with `@warn_unused_result` is that it is only helpful if you apply the attribute to all of the relevant places (i.e. it is a proactive strategy on your part). If you forget to add the attribute, then no warnings will be sent. In Swift 3, the logic is reversed and you now get a warning on unused results by default. If you want to explicitly let the compiler know that the return value can safely be ignored, you can use the `@discardableResult` attribute. Here is an example that demonstrates its usage.

```
@discardableResult
func complexFunctionNonEssentialResult()->Int{
    // do complex logic
    // return trivial status code
    return 123
}
```

In Swift 3, the mutating method `sortInPlace()` became `sort()` and the non-mutating version changed from `sort()` to `sorted()`.

You can read more about the proposal at
https://github.com/apple/swift-evolution/blob/master/proposals/0047-nonvoid-warn.md

Removing var from function parameter lists [SE-0003]

Using var in a function parameter list was valid in Swift 2. Since parameter types are immutable by default, developers attempted to use var in the parameter list to pass a mutable parameter to their function implementation. While you could do this in Swift, it actually proved to be a fairly useless tactic. Let me explain. Yes, you can use the var keyword to pass a mutable variant to your function body. However, any changes you make to the variable are not propagated back to the original type. Therefore, you are using a mutable copy that is scoped to the function's body. Let's examine how this works in practice with an example:

```
func booyah(howHigh: Int){
    howHigh += 100 // -> illegal assignment
}

func booyahTake2(var yaFeelMe: Int){
    yaFeelMe += 100   // -> legal but doesn't write back to caller
}
```

You could have, just as easily, accomplished the same objective by assigning the passed in parameter to a local copy within the function body. See below for the equivalent function definition:

```
func booyahTake3(yaFeelMe: Int){
    var yaFeelMe = yaFeelMe
    yaFeelMe += 100
}
```

Finally, many developers were confusing var parameters with those marked as inout. Either version will give a mutable local copy but only the inout variant will propagate changes back to function caller. Given the overall confusion, var as a parameter modifier has been removed in Swift 3. In the following example, the howManyTimes variable is updated with its value propagated back to the function caller because it is marked as an inout parameter:

```
func trifecta(inout howManyTimes: Int){
    howManyTimes += 2000  // updates the actual passed in variable
}
```

You can read the proposal at
https://github.com/apple/swift-evolution/blob/master/proposals/0003-remove-var-parameters.md

Removing ++ and — operators [SE-0004]

The increment (++) and decrement (--) operators were added to Swift because they existed in C. In addition, many developers coming to Swift are used to seeing them in the other languages. Let's examine how these operators work and then we can cover the gotchas.

```
var row = 0
let currentRow = ++row    // pre - adds 1 to row than assigns new value
let nextRow = row++        // post - assigns than adds 1 from row
let previousRow = --row    // pre - minus 1 from row than assigns to value
let backOneRow = row--     // post - assigns than subtracts 1 from row
```

Disadvantages /Gotchas:

- It's easy to get the pre and post part of the increment/decrement operator wrong, which gives you an incorrect output
- The syntax is shorthand for += or -=, which doesn't save you that many keystrokes over += 1 or -= 1
- The operators are largely used in C style for...loops, where the return value is ignored. Since we have for...loops loops, ranges, maps, and enumerate/iterate functions, we don't need these operators
- You can only use these operators with a small set of types (such as integers and floating point scalars)
- If you are learning your first programming language, these operators increase the amount of stuff you have to learn without providing meaningful value you couldn't get through other features that Swift offers

Essentially, the Swift team felt the disadvantages of keeping these operators outweighed the advantages and opted to remove them in Swift 3.

You can read the proposal here:
https://github.com/apple/swift-evolution/blob/master/proposals/0004-remove-pre-post-inc-decrement.md

Removing C-style for loops [SE-0007]

Similar to the increment and decrement operators we just discussed, the C-style `for...in` loop also seems to have been added to Swift for its C language ancestry. Swift offers several *Swifty* conventions for iterating and looping that are better options than the C-style loop. In fact, C-style loops really aren't used all that much. Once a developer starts to master Swift concepts, the developer generally chooses not to use C-style loops. When considering the iteration of a collection, `for...in` loops are considerably harder to implement than `for...in` statements. Finally, if C-style `for` loops did not already exist in Swift; no one would miss them or beg for their inclusion into the language. With Swift 3, C-style for loops are officially eliminated from the language.

 You can read more about the proposal at
https://github.com/apple/swift-evolution/blob/master/proposals/0
007-remove-c-style-for-loops.md

Removing implicit tuple splat from functions [SE-0029]

In previous versions of Swift, function calls allowed developers to pass an argument list in the form of a tuple, commonly referred to as a *tuple splat*. A *tuple splat* could be defined in one place and then passed to a function as one object, removing the need to pass individual arguments to a function. Let's take a look at an example to make this concept clearer.

```
func fooTastic(members: [String], instruments:[String]){
    // fantastic work happening here...
}

let foo = (["Jackson", "Carey", "Wonderland"], instruments:["drums",
"bass", "keyboard"])
fooTastic(foo)
```

In our example, we create the `fooTastic()` function to accept two String array arguments. We then created a tuple that encapsulates the arguments we want to pass to our function. Last, we call `fooTastic()` passing in our foo tuple. This works, but here are some disadvantages to consider:

- Our `foo` tuple has to mirror the way the arguments are represented in the function: meaning we have to drop the members parameter label. We must include the instruments label in our tuple or the compiler will complain when we pass the tuple as an argument.

- Passing just a tuple to the function makes our method appear to have overloads, which is confusing to anyone tasked with maintaining this code.
- The current implement of tuple splats is inconsistent and buggy in terms of implementation.

All things considered, we just don't need this added complexity in the language and hence this feature has been removed from Swift 3.

 You can read more about the proposal at
https://github.com/apple/swift-evolution/blob/master/proposals/0
029-remove-implicit-tuple-splat.md

Adjusting inout declarations for type decoration [SE-0031]

This is a minor change for Swift 3. The *inout* keyword has been moved to the right of the colon (:) and next to the type in function definitions. Nothing has changed about how inout variables behave in code. You are still giving the parameter decorated with inout the ability to mutate the value within the body of the function. The change is meant to move the decoration name closer to the type it is actually modifying. Since we are modifying the type and not the label, it makes more sense for the keyword to be next to the type.

In Swift 2:

```
func trifecta(inout howManyTimes: Int){
    howManyTimes += 2000
}
```

In Swift 3:

```
func trifecta(howManyTimes: inout Int){
    howManyTimes += 2000
}
```

 You can read the proposal at
https://github.com/apple/swift-evolution/blob/master/proposals/0
031-adjusting-inout-declarations.md

Replacing equal signs with colons for attribute arguments [SE-0040]

As we discussed in *[SE-0047]*, attributes are special constructs that you apply to a declaration or type. You specify an attribute using the @ symbol followed by a name and optionally any attribute arguments in parentheses:

```
@<attribute name>
@<attribute name>(attribute arguments)
```

Unlike regular functions and parameter labels, you use = instead of a colon to separate the argument name from its value. This is inconsistent with our standard mode of operation in the rest of Swift. Therefore, in Swift 3, attribute arguments will receive the same treatment as other Swift arguments, using the colon over and equal sign.

In Swift 2:

```
@warn_unused_result(mutable_variant="sortInPlace")
    public func sort() -> [Self.Generator.Element]
```

In Swift 3:

```
@available(*, deprecated, renamed: "NSUnderlyingErrorKey")
    public static let underlyingErrorKey: ErrorUserInfoKey
```

 You can read the proposal at
https://github.com/apple/swift-evolution/blob/master/proposals/0
040-attributecolons.md

Standardizing function type argument syntax to require parentheses [SE-0066]

Functions are defined in Swift to use parentheses to enclose their argument lists. The purpose is to make it clear where the function declaration begins and ends. However, Swift 2 allowed you to call a function, under certain conditions, without using the parentheses. Let's look at an example to make this concept clearer. In the following example, we define functions using parentheses and their equivalents by dropping the parentheses:

```
let a: (Int) -> Int
let b: (Int) -> (Int)-> Int
```

This can also be written without parentheses as:

```
let a1: Int -> Int
var b1: Int -> Int -> Int
```

Granted, the second form is a bit shorter since it omits the parentheses. However, the trade-off introduces code that is not consistent with the way the function types are defined in the rest of the language. Frankly, you don't get any real value or expressive components by omitting the parentheses. Crafting function types this way is only syntactic sugar with no substance. In Swift 3, you will no longer be able to use this shortcut form when defining function types.

 You can read more about the proposal at
https://github.com/apple/swift-evolution/blob/master/proposals/0066-standardize-function-type-syntax.md

Enforcing the order of defaulted parameters [SE-0060]

Order matters when you call a function in Swift, but there is one exception to this rule for functions that contain parameters with default arguments. Under this edge case, you can call this type of function using only a portion of the argument names. Let's look at some examples of how you can call a function that contains default parameters.

In Swift 2:

```
func shifty(arg1: String = "", arg2: String = "", arg3: Int = 1){}
```

The first way to call the `shifty()` function is to use all of the default parameters, meaning we don't pass anything at the call site. This is valid in Swift 2 and is generally expected behavior. See below for an example using just the function with all default parameter values:

```
shifty()
```

Another way to call the `shifty()` would be to omit the arguments we don't care about and only pass in the ones we do. We could pass in just one argument such as arg2 or arg3 and our function would continue to work. In the following example, we demonstrate calling our shifty function while omitting some of the parameters:

```
shifty(arg2: "")
shifty(arg3: 3)
```

Finally, we could call the function with multiple arguments. See below for example usage of the shifty function with multiple arguments:

```
shifty(arg2: "", arg3: 3)

shifty("", arg3: 3)

shifty(arg2: "", arg3: 4)
```

Allowing this behavior is actually a bit confusing to developers and goes against the strict ordering that is enforced throughout the rest of the language. Swift 3 removes this behavior and forces you to maintain the parameter ordering when using default parameters. Let's see how our `shifty()` function works now in Swift 3.

In Swift 3:

```
func shifty(arg1: String = "arg1", arg2: String = "arg2", arg3: Int = 0){}
```

There is no change to how we call a function using all defaulted arguments:

```
shifty()
```

When we call a function with just one argument, we have to use the argument label for our parameter. The other difference is that we can not just call the arguments in any order we choose. We can omit defaulted parameters but we can not call them in any order we choose. Let's examine some of the ways we can call our `shifty()` function in Swift 3.

```
shifty(arg1: "") // valid
shifty(arg2: "") // valid
    shifty(arg3: 3)    //valid
    shifty(arg3: 3, arg1: "test")    //invalid!
```

If you think about this for a while, I bet you could see why the Swift team made this change. We sacrifice a shorter syntax for enhanced readability.

 You can read the proposal at
https://github.com/apple/swift-evolution/blob/master/proposals/0060-defaulted-parameter-order.md

Making optional requirements Objective-C only [SE-0070]

Objective-C protocols have a feature that allows the developer to mark some of the behavior as optional. While this makes sense for Objective-C, it would not make sense as a Swift feature. In Swift, the protocol author could provide a default implementation using protocol extensions and protocol inheritance. Similarly, with protocol inheritance, the author could add the optional methods to a separate protocol that a developer could adopt if the optional behavior is of interest and not make it a requirement for all users of the protocol. The main takeaway is that you have better options in Swift for tackling optional protocol requirements and, therefore, adding Objective-C optional features on protocols to Swift is not necessary.

Now that we know why the Swift team opted not to include this as a Swift feature, let's discuss how to handle Objective-C optional in Swift 3. Basically, we use the `@objc` attribute to decorate the parts of the protocol we want to distinguish as an Objective-C only requirement. We also add the optional keyword to each of the function signatures. For the most part, you won't have to change anything on your end in Swift. You also don't have to modify your Objective-C code. The migrator handles all of the work for you.

In Objective-C:

```
@protocol UICollectionViewDataSource <NSObject>
@required

-  (NSInteger)collectionView:(UICollectionView *)collectionView
numberOfItemsInSection:(NSInteger)section;

-  (UICollectionViewCell *)collectionView:(UICollectionView *)collectionView
cellForItemAtIndexPath:(NSIndexPath *)indexPath;

@optional

-  (NSInteger)numberOfSectionsInCollectionView:(UICollectionView
*)collectionView;

-  (UICollectionReusableView *)collectionView:(UICollectionView
*)collectionView viewForSupplementaryElementOfKind:(NSString *)kind
atIndexPath:(NSIndexPath *)indexPath;

-  (BOOL)collectionView:(UICollectionView *)collectionView
canMoveItemAtIndexPath:(NSIndexPath *)indexPath;

-  (void)collectionView:(UICollectionView *)collectionView
moveItemAtIndexPath:(NSIndexPath *)sourceIndexPath
```

```
toIndexPath:(NSIndexPath*)destinationIndexPath;

@end


Swift
public protocol UICollectionViewDataSource : NSObjectProtocol {

public func collectionView(_ collectionView: UICollectionView,
numberOfItemsInSection section: Int) -> Int

public func collectionView(_ collectionView: UICollectionView,
cellForItemAt indexPath: IndexPath) -> UICollectionViewCell

optional public func numberOfSections(in collectionView: UICollectionView)
-> Int

optional public func collectionView(_ collectionView: UICollectionView,
viewForSupplementaryElementOfKind kind: String, at indexPath: IndexPath) ->
UICollectionReusableView

optional public func collectionView(_ collectionView: UICollectionView,
canMoveItemAt indexPath: IndexPath) -> Bool

optional public func collectionView(_ collectionView: UICollectionView,
moveItemAt sourceIndexPath: IndexPath, to destinationIndexPath: IndexPath)
}
```

Our code snippets above show the Objective-C protocol (with optional methods) and the Swift version once it is passed through the migrator.

 You can read the proposal at
https://github.com/apple/swift-evolution/blob/master/proposals/0
070-optional-requirements.md

Summary

In this chapter we covered how functions are created and called. We touched on several features that weren't very *Swifty* and have been removed in Swift 3. We also explored attributes and attribute arguments, focusing on syntax changes, and new additions and subtractions from the language. In the next chapter, we will do a deep dive into closures and collections.

6
Extra, Extra Collection and Closure Changes That Rock!

In this chapter, we are focusing on collection and closure changes in Swift 3. Collections are important to all programming languages because they allow you hold groups of related items. Closures are also important to Swift because they give you the ability to pass around functionality to be used in a different location of your code. There are several nice additions that will make working with collections even more fun. We will also explore some of the confusing side effects of creating closures in Swift 2.2 and how those have been fixed in Swift 3.

Collection and sequence type changes

Let's begin our discussion with Swift 3 changes to Collection and Sequence types. Some of the changes are subtle and others are bound to require a decent amount of refactoring to your custom implementations. Swift provides three main collection types for warehousing your values: arrays, dictionaries, and sets. Arrays allow you to store values in an ordered list. Dictionaries provide unordered key-value storage for your data. Finally, sets provide an unordered list of unique values (that is, no duplicates allowed).

Lazy FlatMap for sequence of optional [SE-0008]

Arrays, dictionaries, and sets are implemented as generic types in Swift. They each implement the new Collection protocol, which implements the Sequence protocol. Along this path from top-level type to Sequence protocol, you will find various other protocols that are also implemented in this inheritance chain. For our discussion on `flatMap` and lazy `flatMap` changes, I want to focus on Sequences.

Sequences contain a group of values that allow the user to visit each value one at a time. In Swift, you might consider using a for-in loop to iterate through your collection. The Sequence protocol provides implementations of many operations that you might want to perform on a list using sequential access; all of which you can override when you adopt the protocol in your custom collections. One such operation is the flatMap function, which returns an array containing the flattened, or rather concatenated, values resulting from a transforming operation applied to each element of the sequence. Let's consider how we could use the flatMap method.

```
let scores = [0, 5, 6, 8, 9]
          .flatMap{ [$0, $0 * 2] }
print(scores)  // [0, 0, 5, 10, 6, 12, 8, 16, 9, 18]
```

In our example above, we take a list of scores and call flatMap with our transforming closure. Each value is converted into a sequence containing the original value and a doubled value. Once the transforming operations complete, the flatMap method flattens the intermediate sequences into a single sequence.

We can also use the flatMap method with *Sequences* that contain optional values to accomplish a similar outcome. This time we are omitting values from the Sequence we flatten by return nil on the transformation. In the next example, we use the flatMap method to remove all nil values from our collection.

```
let oddSquared = [1, 2, 3, 4, 5, 10].flatMap { n in
    n % 2 == 1 ? n*n : nil
}
print(oddSquared) // [1, 9, 25]
```

The previous two examples were fairly basic transformations on small sets of values. In a more complex situation, the collections that you need to work with might be very large with expensive transformation operations. Under those parameters, you would not want to perform the flatMap operation or any other costly operation until it was absolutely needed. Luckily, in Swift we have lazy operations for this use case. Sequences contain a lazy property that returns a LazySequence that can perform lazy operations on Sequence methods. Using our first example above, we can obtain a lazy sequence and call flatMap to get a lazy implementation. Only in the lazy scenario, the operation isn't completed until scores is used sometime later in code. To demonstrate lazy operations, we define a collection that uses the lazy property with our flatMap method.

```
let scores    [0, 5, 6, 8, 9]
    .lazy
    .flatMap{ [$0, $0 * 2] } // lazy assignment has not executed

for score in scores{
```

```
        print(score)
    }
```

The `lazy` operation works as we would expect in our test above. However, when we use the `lazy` form of `flatMap` with our second example that contains optionals, our `flatMap` executes immediately in Swift 2. Using the lazy version of `oddSquared` should delay execution of our `flatMap` operation until we use the variable. However, the `flatMap` method executes immediately, as if the lazy form didn't exist..

```
let oddSquared = [1, 2, 3, 4, 5, 10]
    .lazy              // lazy assignment but has not executed
    .flatMap { n in
    n % 2 == 1 ? n*n : nil
}

for odd in oddSquared{
    print(odd)
}
```

Essentially, this was a feature in Swift that has been changed in Swift 3 to behave similar to other lazy implementations.

 You can read the proposal at the following link `https://github.com/app le/swift-evolution/blob/master/proposals/8-lazy-flatmap-for-op tionals.md`

Adding a first(where:) method to Sequence [SE-0032]

A common task for working with collections is to find the first element that matches a condition. An example would be to ask for the first student in an array of students whose test scores contain 100. You could accomplish this by using a predicate to return the filtered sequence that matched the criteria and then just give back the first student in the sequence. However, it would be much easier to just call a single method that could return the item without the two-step approach. This functionality was missing in Swift 2, but was voted in by the community and has been added for this release. In Swift 3 there is now a method on the Sequence protocol to implement `first(where:)`.

```
["Jack", "Roger", "Rachel", "Joey"].first { (name) -> Bool in
name.contains("Ro")
} // =>returns Roger
```

This `first(where:)` extension is a nice addition to the language because it ensures that a simple and common task is actually easy to perform in Swift.

 You can read the proposal at the following link `https://github.com/app le/swift-evolution/blob/master/proposals/32-sequencetype-find. md`

Add sequence(first: next:) and sequence(state: next:) [SE-0094]

Swift 3 introduces two new global functions that operate on sequences: `sequence(first:next:)`

and `(state:next:)`.

Let's look at the full definitions below:

```
public func sequence<T>(first: T, next: @escaping (T) -> T?) ->
UnfoldSequence<T, (T?, Bool)>

public func sequence<T, State>(state: State, next: @escaping (inout State)
-> T?) -> UnfoldSequence<T, State>

public struct UnfoldSequence<Element, State> : Sequence, IteratorProtocol
```

These two functions were added as replacements to the C-style for loops that were removed in Swift 3 and to serve as a compliment to the global reduce function that already exists in Swift 2. What's interesting about the additions is that each function has the capability of generating and working with infinite sized sequences. Let's examine the first sequence function to get a better understanding of how it works:

```
/// - Parameter first: The first element to be returned from the sequence.
/// - Parameter next: A closure that accepts the previous sequence element
and
///    returns the next element.
/// - Returns: A sequence that starts with `first` and continues with every
///    value returned by passing the previous element to `next`.
///
func sequence<T>(first: T, next: @escaping (T) -> T?) -> UnfoldSequence<T,
(T?, Bool)>
```

The first sequence method returns a sequence that is created from repeated invocations of the *next* parameter, which holds a closure that will be lazily executed. The return value is an UnfoldSequence that contains the first parameter passed to the sequence method plus the result of applying the *next* closure on the previous value. The sequence is finite if next eventually returns nil and is infinite if next never returns *nil*. In the example that follows, we create and assign our sequence using the trailing closure form of sequence(first: next:).

```
let mysequence = sequence(first: 1.1) { $0 < 2 ? $0 + 0.1 : nil }
for x in mysequence{
    print (x)
} // 1.1 1.2 1.3 1.4 1.5 1.6 1.7 1.8 1.9 2.0
```

Our finite sequence will begin with 1.1 and will call next repeatedly until our next result is greater than 2 at which case next will return nil. We could easily convert this to an infinite sequence by removing our condition that our previous value must not be greater than 2. The second sequence function maintains mutable state that is passed to all lazy calls of next to create and return a sequence. Let's consider an example using the second method:

```
/// - Parameter state: The initial state that will be passed to the
closure.
/// - Parameter next: A closure that accepts an `inout` state and returns
the
///    next element of the sequence.
/// - Returns: A sequence that yields each successive value from `next`.
///
public func sequence<T, State>(state: State, next: (inout State) -> T?) ->
UnfoldSequence<T, State>
```

This version of the sequence function uses a passed in closure that allows you to update the mutable state each time next is called. As was the case with our first sequence function, a finite sequence ends when next returns a nil. You can turn a finite sequence into an infinite one by never returning nil when next is called.

Let's create an example of how this version of the sequence method might be used. Traversing a hierarchy of views with nested views or any list of nested types is a perfect task for using the second version of the sequence function. Let's create a an Item class that has two properties. A name property and an optional parent property to keep track of the item's owner. The ultimate owner will not have a parent, meaning the parent property will be nil.

Let's define an Item class to use in our example to demonstrate usage of these new concepts.

```
class Item{
    var parent: Item?
    var name: String = ""
}
```

Next, we create a parent and two nested children items. Parent of `child1` will be the parent item and parent of `child2` will be `child1`.

```
let parent = Item()
parent.name = "parent"

let child1 = Item()
child1.name = "child1"
child1.parent = parent

let child2 = Item()
child2.name = "child2"
child2.parent = child1
```

Now it's time to create our sequence. The sequence needs two parameters from us: a `state` parameter and a `next` closure. I made the state an `Item` with an initial value of `child2`. The reason for this is because I want to start at the lowest leaf of my tree and traverse to the ultimate parent. Our example only has three levels, but you could have lots of levels in a more complex example. As for the *next* parameter, I'm using a closure expression that expects a mutable Item as its state. My closure will also return an optional Item. In the body of our closure, I use our current Item (mutable state parameter) to access the Item's parent. I update the state and return the parent.

```
let itemSeq = sequence(state: child2, next: {
    (next: inout Item)->Item? in
    let parent = next.parent
    next = parent != nil ? parent! : next
    return parent
})


for item in itemSeq{
    print("name: \(item.name)")
}
```

There are some gotchas here that I want to address so that you will better understand how to define your own next closure for this sequence method.

- The state parameter could really be anything you want it to be. It's for your benefit in helping you determine the next element of the sequence and to give you relevant information about where you are in the sequence. One idea to improve our example above would be to track how many levels of nesting we have. We could have made our state a tuple that contained an integer counter for the nesting level along with the current item.
- The next closure needs to be expanded to show the signature. Because of Swift's expressiveness and conciseness when it comes to closures, you might be tempted to convert the *next* closure into a shorter form and omit the signature. Do not do this unless your *next* closure is extremely simple and you are positive that the compiler will be able to infer your types. Your code will be harder to maintain when you use the short closure format and you won't get extra points for style when someone else inherits it.
- Don't forget to update your state parameter in the body of your closure. This really is your best chance to know where you are in your sequence. Forgetting to update the state will probably cause you to get unexpected results when you try to step through your sequence.
- Make a clear decision ahead of time about whether you are creating a finite or infinite sequence. This decision is evident in how you return from your next closure. An infinite sequence is not bad to have when you are expecting it, however, if you iterate over this sequence using a `for...in` loop, you could get more than you bargained for, provided you were assuming this loop would end.

A new model for collections and indices [SE-0065]

Swift 3 introduces a new model for collections that moves the responsibility of the index traversal from the index to the collection itself. To make this a reality for collections, the Swift team introduced four areas of change:

- The Index property of a collection can be any type that implements the *Comparable* protocol
- Swift removes any distinction between intervals and ranges; leaving just ranges
- Private index traversal methods are now public
- Changes to ranges make closed ranges work without the potential for errors

You can read the proposal at the following link `https://github.com/app`
`le/swift-evolution/blob/master/proposals/65-collections-move-i`
`ndices.md`

Introducing the Collection protocol

In Swift 3, Foundation collection types such as Arrays, Dictionaries, and Sets are generic types that implement the newly created Collection protocol. This change was needed in order to support traversal on the collection. If you want to create custom collections of your own, you will need to understand the Collection protocol and where it lives in the Collection protocol hierarchy. We are going to cover the important aspects to the new collection model to ease you transition and to get your ready to create custom collection types of your own.

The Collection protocol builds on the Sequence protocol to provide methods for accessing specific elements when using a collection. For example, you can use a collection's `index(_:offsetBy:)` method to return an index that is a specified distance away from the reference index.

```
let numbers = [10, 20, 30, 40, 50, 60]
let twoAheadIndex = numbers.index(numbers.startIndex, offsetBy: 2)
print(numbers[twoAheadIndex]) //=> 30
```

In our example above, we create the `twoAheadIndex` constant to hold the position in our numbers collection that is two positions away from our starting index. We simply use this index to retrieve the value from our collection using subscript notation.

Conforming to the Collection protocol

If you would like to create your own custom collections, you need to adopt the Collection protocol by declaring `startIndex` and `endIndex` properties, a subscript to support access to your elements, and the `index(after: )` method to facilitate traversing your collection's indices.

When we are migrating existing types over to Swift 3, the migrator has some known issues with converting custom collections. It's likely that you can easily resolve the compiler issues by checking the imported types for conformance to the Collection protocol.

Additionally, you need to conform to the Sequence and IndexableBase protocols as the Collection protocol adopts them both.

```
public protocol Collection : Indexable, Sequence { ... }
```

A simple custom collection could look like the following example. Notice that I have defined my `Index` type to be an `Int`. In Swift 3, you define the index to be any type that implements the Comparable protocol:

```
struct MyCollection<T>: Collection{
    typealias Index = Int
    var startIndex: Index
    var endIndex: Index
    var _collection: [T]
    subscript (position: Index) -> T{
        return _collection[position]
    }
    func index(after i: Index) -> Index {
        return i + 1
    }
    init(){
        startIndex = 0
        endIndex = 0
        _collection = []
    }
    mutating func add(item: T){
        _collection.append(item)
    }
}

var myCollection: MyCollection<String> = MyCollection()
myCollection.add(item: "Harry")
myCollection.add(item: "William")
myCollection[0]
```

The Collection protocol has default implementations for most of its methods, the Sequence protocols methods, and the IndexableBase protocols methods. This means you are only required to provide a few things of your own. You can, however, implement as many of the other methods that make sense for your collection.

New Range and associated indices types

Swift 2's `Range<T>`, `ClosedInterval<T>`, and `OpenInterval<T>` are going away in Swift 3. These types are being replaced with four new types. Two of the new range types support general ranges with bounds that implement the Comparable protocol: `Range<T>` and `ClosedRange<T>`. The other two range types conform to `RandomAccessCollection`. These types support ranges whose bounds implement the Strideable protocol.

Last, ranges are no longer iterable since ranges are now represented as a pair of indices. To keep legacy code working, the Swift team introduced an associated Indices type, which is iterable. In addition, three generic types were created to provide a default *Indices* type for each type of collection traversal category. The generics are `DefaultIndices<C>`, `DefaultBidirectionalIndices<C>`, and `DefaultRandomAccessIndices<C>`; each stores its underlying collection for traversal.

Quick takeaways

I covered a lot of stuff in a just a few pages on collection types in Swift 3. Here are the highlights to keep in mind about the collections and indices.

- Collection types (built-in and custom) implement the Collection protocol.
- Iterating over collections has moved to the Collection – the index no longer has that ability.
- You can create your own collections by adopting the Collection protocol. You need to implement:
  - `startIndex` and `endIndex` properties,
  - The subscript method to support access to your elements
  - And the `index(after: )` method to facilitate traversing your collection's indices.

Closure changes for Swift 3

A closure in Swift is a block of code that can be used in a function call as a parameter or assigned to a variable to execute their functionality at a later time. Closures are a core feature to Swift and are familiar to developers that are new to Swift as they may remind them of lambda functions in other programming languages. For Swift 3, there were two notable changes that I will highlight in this section. The first change deals with inout captures. The second is a change that makes non-escaping closures the default.

Limiting inout Capture of @noescape Closures [SE-0035]

In Swift 2, capturing inout parameters in an escaping closure is difficult for developers to understand. Some closures are assigned to variables and then passed to functions as arguments. If the function that contains the closure parameter returns from its call and the passed in closure is used later, then you have an escaping closure. On the other hand, if the closure is only used within the function to which it is passed and not used later, then you have a non-escaping closure. The distinction is important here because of the mutating nature of inout parameters.

When we pass an inout parameter to a closure, there is a possibility that we will not get the result we expect due to how the inout parameter is stored. The inout parameter is captured as a shadow copy and is only written back to the original if the value changes. This works fine most of the time. However, when the closure is called at a later time (that is, when it escapes), we don't get the result we expect. Our shadow copy can't write back to the original. Let's look at an example.

```
var seed = 10
let simpleAdderClosure = { (inout seed: Int)->Int in
    seed += 1
    return seed * 10
}

var result = simpleAdderClosure(&seed)   //=> seed = 11; result = 110
print(seed) // => 11
```

In the example above, we get what we expect. We have created a closure to increment our passed in inout parameter and then return the new parameter multiplied by 10. When we check the value of *seed* after the closure is called, we see that the value has increased to 11.

In our second example, we modify our closure to return a function instead of just an Int value. We move our logic to the closure that we are defining as our return value.

```
let modifiedClosure = { (inout seed: Int)-> (Int)->Int in
    return { (Int)-> Int in
        seed += 1
        return seed * 10
    }
}

print(seed)   //=> 11
var resultFn = modifiedClosure(&seed)
var result = resultFn(1)
```

```
print(seed) // => 11
```

This time when we execute the `modifiedClosure` with our `seed` value we get a function as the result. After executing this intermediate function, we check our *seed* value and see that the value is unchanged; even though we are still incrementing the `seed` value.

These two slight differences in syntax when using `inout` parameters generate different results. Without knowledge of how shadow copy works, it would be hard to understand the difference in results. Ultimately, this is just another situation where you receive more harm than good by allowing this feature to remain in the language.

 You can read the proposal at the following link `https://github.com/app le/swift-evolution/blob/master/proposals/35-limit-inout-captur e.md`

Resolution

In Swift 3, the compiler now limits `inout` parameter usage with closures to non-escaping (`@noescape`). You will receive an error if the compiler detects that your closure escapes when it contains `inout` parameters.

Making non-escaping closures the default [SE-0103]

In previous versions of Swift, the default behavior of function parameters whose type was a closure was to allow escaping. This made sense as most of the Objective-C blocks (closures in Swift) imported into Swift were escaping. The delegation pattern in Objective-C, as implemented as blocks, was composed of delegate blocks that escaped. So why would the Swift team want to change the default to non-escaping as the default? Let's look at examples in Swift 2.2 and Swift 3 to get a better understanding of why this change makes sense.

In Swift 2.2:

```
var callbacks:[String : ()->String] = [:]
func myEscapingFunction(name:String, callback:()->String){
    callbacks[name] = callback
}
myEscapingFunction("cb1", callback: {"just another cb"})
for cb in callbacks{
    print("name: \(cb.0) value: \(cb.1())")
```

```
    }
```

In Swift 3:

```
    var callbacks:[String : ()->String] = [:]
    func myEscapingFunction(name:String, callback: @escaping ()->String){
        callbacks[name] = callback
    }
    myEscapingFunction(name:"cb1", callback: {"just another cb"})
    for cb in callbacks{
        print("name: \(cb.0) value: \(cb.1())")
    }
```

The Swift team believes you can write better functional algorithms with non-escaping closures. An additional supporting factor is the change to require non-escaping closures when using `inout` parameters with the closure *[SE-0035]*. All things considered, this change will likely have little impact on your code. When the compiler detects that you are attempting to create an escaping closure, you will get a warning that you are possibly creating an escaping closure. You can easily correct the error by adding `@escaping` or via the `fixit` that accompanies the error.

 You can read the proposal at the following link `https://github.com/app le/swift-evolution/blob/master/proposals/13-make-noescape-defa ult.md`

Summary

In this chapter we covered changes to collections and closures. We learned about the new Collection protocol that forms the base of the new collection model and how to adopt the protocol in our own custom collections. The new collection model made a significant change in moving collection traversal from the index to the collection itself. The new collection model changes are necessary in order to support Objective-C interactivity and to provide a mechanism to iterate over the collections items using the collections itself. As for closures, we also explored the motivation for the language moving to non-escaping closures as the default. We also learned how to properly use `inout` parameters with closures in Swift 3. In the next chapter, we are will cover more type changes and type aliases within protocols and protocol extensions.

7
Hold onto Your Chair; Advanced Type Changes Are Here!

Swift is a great language, and it's getting better with each release. So far, we've covered most of the functionality that you are likely to use in your everyday projects. We are going to cover a few improvements to the language that you might not use on a regular basis. This chapter focuses on `UnsafePointer` types, `typealiases`, and floating point operations.

Unmanaged and UnsafePointer changes

Brace yourself, because we are about to skim the surface of a few types that you may not have seen a lot of and whose names scream, *I'll pass on those* for the squeamish among you. For the most part, the naming conventions for types in Swift seem approachable and sane to the average developer. However, there is a subset of types that aren't even listed in the main sections of the Swift Programming language document. These are the *black sheep* types of the language. The ones with names such as `Unmanaged`, `UnsafeMutableRawPointer`, and `UnsafeBufferPointer`. These types just feel `unsafe` to use. Perhaps, the names are a big hint that you, as the developer, need to take some precautions when using these types. If you develop long enough in Swift, you will eventually come across one of these types. We might as well cover the changes for these types in Swift 3 so that you will be armed with the most current knowledge of how to use the new features when you need them.

Changing Unmanaged to use UnsafePointer [SE-0017]

Unmanaged is a type in Swift that allows you to work with an unmanaged object reference, meaning you are responsible for the object's memory and for keeping it alive. An UnsafePointer is a type that represents a raw pointer to data of type pointer. You are fully responsible for managing memory with this type. Both types are useful when dealing with C APIs. C functions that accept types such as void * or const void * are extremely common but can present issues in Swift.

When a C API passes a void * or const void * type (or others that aren't easily coerced into a Foundation type) to Swift, the type is converted to an UnsafePointer. This is our first step, but not our final destination in terms of getting a type that we can use efficiently in Swift. We ultimately want an Unmanaged type because this type provides a type-safe wrapper around our object, even though it does not participate in **Automatic Reference Counting** (**ARC**). With an Unmanaged type, the developer can manually make memory decisions. In Swift 2, there was no direct conversion to allow you to go from UnsafePointer to Unmanaged type. You had to convert to a **bridge type** first and then convert to your preferred type at **UnsafePointer** | **COpaquePointer** | **Unmanaged.**

You accomplished the conversions using one of the following methods on the Unmanaged type:

```
static func fromOpaque(value: COpaquePointer) -> Unmanaged<Instance>
func toOpaque() -> COpaquePointer
```

In Swift 2:

```
let str0: CFString = "Test string" as CFString
let bits: Unmanaged<CFString> = Unmanaged.passRetained(str0)
let oPtr: COpaquePointer = bits.toOpaque()
let ptr: UnsafePointer<CFString> = UnsafePointer(oPtr)

let oPtr2 = COpaquePointer(ptr)
let str1: Unmanaged<CFString> = Unmanaged.fromOpaque(oPtr2)
str1.takeRetainedValue()
```

In Swift 3, we can now convert directly between Unmanaged and UnsafePointer. The fromOpaque and toOpaque methods replace COpaquePointer with UnsafeRawPointer and UnsafeMutableRawPointer types. We essentially streamlined our code by eliminating the middleman.

```
static func fromOpaque(_ value: UnsafeRawPointer) -> Unmanaged<Instance>
func toOpaque() -> UnsafeMutableRawPointer
```

In Swift 3:

```
let str0: CFString = "Test string" as CFString
let bits = Unmanaged.passUnretained(str0)
let ptr = bits.toOpaque()

let str1: Unmanaged<CFString> = Unmanaged.fromOpaque(ptr)
str1.takeRetainedValue()
```

You can read the proposal at https://github.com/apple/swift-evolut
ion/blob/master/proposals/17-convert-unmanaged-to-use-unsafepo
inter.md.

Making UnsafePointer explicit using Optional [SE-0055]

Unlike in Objective-C, where you can mark pointers as `nullable` or `nonnull`, Swift does not have a way to determine if a pointer is null. Therefore, when you obtain a reference to an `UnsafePointer<T>`, you could be holding a pointer to null. This is an issue because an `UnsafePointer` (and similar types) are essentially referencing C pointers. If the developer's code is not expecting or accounting for null values, then the program could crash. This is particularly troubling in Swift due to the fact that every non-trivial operation you could perform using an `UnsafePointer` relies on a valid underlying pointer that is not null.

Fortunately, we don't have to deal with this in Swift for built-in types, classes, and structures, because we have optionals. As we know, `optionals` let us deal with situations in which our type may or may not contain a value. New in Swift 3, we can apply `optionals` to `UnsafePointer` types. When you know for sure that your pointer can't be null, you use the regular form: `UnsafePointer<T>`. When you want to represent a `nullable` version, you use the optional syntax (`UnsafePointer<T>?`).

You can read the proposal at https://github.com/apple/swift-evolut
ion/blob/master/proposals/55-optional-unsafe-pointers.md.

Adding UnsafeRawPointer [SE-0107]

Swift added the `UnsafePointer` type to interoperate with C APIs and to facilitate building high performance data structures (think low-level graphics programming or heavy math-based modeling). In this respect, `UnsafePointer` is an important addition to Swift. Unfortunately, the implementation of `UnsafePointer` allows the developer to bypass the safety measures put in place to ensure type safe memory access. It's possible to use `UnsafePointer` types to violate compiler logic. The violation would normally cause a compilation error. However, the compiler has a built-in exception for the `UnsafePointer` type and allows the compilation to proceed. In many cases, running a program that uses the typed memory access to reference a memory location of a different type will cause that program to crash. Swift 3 introduces `UnsafeRawPointer` to deal with un-typed memory. Let's use an example to illustrate type memory access abuse.

In Swift 2:

```
let msg: CFString = "just a few characters" as CFString
let unmgd: Unmanaged<CFString> = Unmanaged.passRetained(msg)
let ptr: UnsafeMutablePointer<CFString> =
UnsafeMutablePointer(unmgd.toOpaque())
// reassign pointer address with new value
ptr[0] = "testing..." as CFString
// use typed access of Int to access CFSTring memory location
let u = UnsafePointer<Int>(ptr)[0]
```

In our type memory access example, we create an `UnsafeMutablePointer<CFString>` to reference a typed block of memory. Then, we change the value in the first block to a new `CFString`, testing our pointer. Everything is fine so far. Next, we create an `UnsafePointer<Int>` from the existing memory location. Note that we bound our type to an *Int* versus the `CFString` we used in the original pointer. If we use this *Int* pointer, our program could crash. Even though the compiler finds this code to be suspicious, it allows compilation because we are using `UnsafePointer` types, which are on the compiler's exception list for certain types of operations. To correct the problem in our example, we need to use a type that can access memory without needing to know the type. `UnsafeRawPointer` and `UnsafeMutableRawPointer` were introduced in Swift 3 to do this very thing.

Takeaways:

- *Raw* types allow un-typed access to memory; *Typed* versions access memory using their types
- *Raw* access essentially allows C type `memcopy` operations, while *Typed* access follows type aliasing rules

- C types are now imported as `UnsafeMutableRawPointer` and
  `UnsafeRawPointer` when the type isn't clear (for example, `const void *` or
  `void *`) and are imported as `UnsafePointer<T>` and
  `UnsafeMutablePointer<T>` when their type can be determined (for example,
  `const T*`)

> You can read one proposal at `https://github.com/apple/swift-evolut`
> `ion/blob/master/proposals/17-unsaferawpointer.md`.

Type aliases and protocol changes

Type aliases are named types that fill in for existing types in Swift. Once defined, you can
use these types anywhere in your code. Swift 3 now supports type aliases based on
generics. In addition, type aliases are now supported for protocols and protocol extensions.
Speaking of protocols, Swift 3 made a change to protocol use that makes things simpler and
paves the way for expected future changes to this feature. Let's add the new changes more
closely and work through some examples.

Generic type aliases [SE-0048]

Generic type aliases are a new addition for Swift 3. As a reminder, a type alias is a way to
declare a named alias for an existing type in the language. After you create your named
alias, you can use the aliased type in your code just as you would any other type. Generic
type aliases allow you to add type parameters that can be used in defining a generic type.
Let's consider a few examples to show the new possibilities you have with creating type
aliases in Swift 3:

```
typealias ScoreBag<T> = [T]
typealias TriplePointTuple<T> = (T,T,T)
typealias AddPlotter<X:Hashable,Y> = Dictionary<X, Y>
typealias UndoItem<T> = [Date:T]
```

> You can read another proposal at `https://github.com/apple/swift-evo`
> `lution/blob/master/proposals/48-generic-typealias.md`.

You can read the proposal at `https://github.com/apple/swift-evolut` `ion/blob/master/proposals/95-any-as-existential.md`.

In prior versions of Swift, you needed to use the `protocol<...>` syntax when you were defining a type that adhered to multiple protocols. In Swift 3, you now use & between each protocol that your type adopts. This is merely syntactical sugar today, but will serve as the base for defining more generic types in future additions of Swift.

In Swift 2:

```
protocol Driving {}
protocol Parking {}
protocol Braking {}
struct Car: Driving, Parking, Braking {}
let zoomzoom: protocol<Driving, Braking, Parking> = Car()
```

In Swift 3:

```
let zoomzoom: Driving & Braking & Parking = Car()
```

To better convey the intent of a compound type built from individual protocols, the Swift team now prefers using & to a comma for defining multiple protocols on a type.

Type aliases in protocols and protocol extensions [SE-0092]

Swift 2.2 introduced the **associatedtype** keyword to handle associated types in protocols. This change removed the confusion around using the *typealias* keyword because it is now only tasked with defining types. An additional benefit of adding the *associatedtype* keyword is that it allows us to make type aliases in protocols and protocol extensions that are based on the associated types. Looking at the *Sequence* protocol from the standard library, we can see that *Iterator* is defined as an associated type that inherits the *IteratorProtocol*. With Swift 3, I can now add a type alias named *Element* that indirectly references an associated type on the *IteratorProtocol* to make my syntax cleaner. Further, I can use any of the type aliases I create in my protocol with my protocol extensions as well.

In Swift 3:

```
public protocol Sequence {

    associatedtype Iterator : IteratorProtocol
    typealias Element = Iterator.Element

    public func makeIterator() -> Iterator

    func map<T>(_ transform: (Element) throws -> T)
rethrows -> [T]

}
```

In the preceding *Sequence* protocol, I can use my type alias `Element` in the `map()` function. In previous versions of Swift, you would have had to use `Iterator.Element`.

 You can read the proposal at `https://github.com/apple/swift-evolut` `ion/blob/master/proposals/92-typealiases-in-protocols.md`.

Floating point changes

Floating-point types are used to hold fractional numbers. The main floating-point types in the standard library are `Float` and `Double`. The Swift team created a `FloatingPoint` protocol to hold common math operations, making it easier for you to create functions that support all of the floating-point types available. In this section, we will cover additions to the `FloatingPoint` protocol and rounding functions.

Enhanced Floating point protocols [SE-0067]

The current `FloatingPoint` protocol doesn't provide a full set of features to really conform to an IEEE 754 `https://en.wikipedia.org/wiki/IEEE_floating_point#CITEREFIEEE_75` `428` type. The changes to the `FloatingPoint` protocol are meant to expand coverage of the operations that most would expect to be included. A second protocol `BinaryFloatingPoint` (conforms to `FloatingPoint`) has also been added to Swift and will be useful for generic programming.

The `FloatingPoint` protocol now contains most of the IEEE 754 basic operations. The `BinaryFloatingPoint` protocol additionally conforms to `FloatLiteralConvertible`. You can perform normal arithmetic and comparison operations using the `FloatingPoint` protocol and more complex operations that work best using floating-point types that have a fixed radix 2 using the `BinaryFloatingPoint` protocol.

There are many new operations defined on the `FloatingPoint` and `BinaryFloatingPoint` protocols, and I'll leave exploring them to you as a future exercise.

 You can read the proposal at `https://github.com/apple/swift-evolut` `ion/blob/master/proposals/67-floating-point-protocols.md`.

New rounding functions on the FloatingPoint protocol [SE-0113]

The Swift standard library does not have built-in methods to implement rounding functions such as `floor()` or `ceil()`. When you need those methods, you have to import `Darwin` or `Glibc` to access the versions implemented using C. In Swift 3, the Swift team added new rounding methods on the `FloatingPoint` protocol. Rounding and/or converting floating-point types to integers are operations the protocol should handle.

The changes to the `FloatingPoint` protocol consist of adding the `FloatingPointRoundingRule` enumeration and two rounding methods, `round()` and `rounded()`:

```
public func rounded(_ rule: FloatingPointRoundingRule) -> Self
public mutating func round(_ rule: FloatingPointRoundingRule)
public mutating func round()

public enum FloatingPointRoundingRule {
    case toNearestOrAwayFromZero
    case toNearestOrEven
    case up
        case down
    case towardZero
    case awayFromZero
}
```

With the new native implementation of the rounding methods, you will be able to replicate behavior that you get with `ceil` and `floor`, for example:

```
(10.5).rounded(.down) // -> 10.0
(5.2).rounded(.up) // -> 6.0
```

 You can read the proposal at `https://github.com/apple/swift-evolut`
`ion/blob/master/proposals/113-rounding-functions-on-floatingpo`
`int.md`.

Summary

We covered changes to `Unmanaged`, `UnsafePointer`, and similar types used when working with C APIs. You learned about Swift 2's compiler quirk when using these types and how things have improved in Swift 3. Next, we covered type alias changes, their use with protocols, and protocol extensions. Finally, we explored changes to the FloatingPoint protocol. In the next chapter, we cover new additions to the Foundation framework.

8
Oh Goodness! Look What is New in the Foundation Framework

Last year, Apple delivered a great talk on the benefits of using value types and protocol-oriented design patterns in our code. This year with Swift 3, the team at Apple added value types to the Foundation framework. Many of our favorite and heavily used classes now have value type equivalents. We will cover how to use Foundation value types throughout this chapter and have you wondering why value types weren't included with Swift from the beginning!

New to Foundation and made possible by Swift 3, the new measurements and units API `ht tps://developer.apple.com/reference/foundation/nsmeasurement` addresses pain points that have been with Objective-C and Swift developers for a long time. Apple has created an extremely well thought out solution to our problems. We will use several examples to hammer in the concepts so that you will leave this chapter better prepared to handle your measurement challenges in the future.

Mutability and Foundation value types

One of the key concepts of the Swift language is to give developers the ability to control the mutability of their objects. We use `let` to make a value a constant and `var` to make the value a variable. However, certain types, when imported from Objective-C, do not provide easy mutability features. Swift 3 aims to change this by adding a new set of Foundation value types to wrap reference types in order to provide mutable options for developers. In fact, this really isn't all that new as Foundation already uses many value types in both

Objective-C and Swift. Foundation has existing types such as primitives, Enumerations, Option sets, and C structure types that already were value types in previous versions of Swift and Objective-C.

To make the conversion from reference type to value type possible, Swift uses the *copy-on-write* technique for new value types whose underlying data contains more than just simple data. With *copy-on-write*, the value type represents a pointer to shared data and only makes a copy of the data, if there is a request to change the data by one of the references to it. The following table lists the new value types added to the Foundation framework.

Table 1: new value types:

Value type	class Type
AffineTransform	NSAffineTransform
CharacterSet	NSCharacterSet, NSMutableCharacterSet
Data	NSData
Date	NSDate
DateComponents	NSDateComponents
DateInterval (new)	
Decimal	NSDecimal
IndexPath	NSIndexPath
IndexSet	NSIndexSet, NSMutableIndexSet
Measurement (new)	
Notification	NSNotification
PersonNameComponents	NSPersonNameComponents
URL	NSURL
URLComponents	NSURLComponents
URLRequest	NSURLRequest, NSMutableURLRequest
URLQueryItem	NSURLQueryItem
UUID	NSUUID

These new value types work just like their counterparts, with the added value that you can control the mutability in a more transparent way. Some of the new value types are implemented as structure types and will have one or more mutating methods exposed. The good news is that the new Foundation value types will have no impact on existing Objective-C code. However, there will be an impact on the Swift side. Any existing Swift code migrated to Swift 3 that uses reference types will shift to call the new value types. While the migrator will do much of the heavy lifting, you will still have opportunities to further enhance your code use. This is because the migrator utilizes a strategy of making the minimum number of changes possible. As an example, the migrator will not attempt to change any Swift subclasses for reference types.

Value types versus reference types

As a refresher, let's quickly cover the difference between value and reference types. Value types hold values and copy content on assignment or when they are passed to methods as a parameter.

```
let avg1: Double = 98.1
var avg2 = avg1
avg2 += 1.2    // -> 99.3
```

In the preceding example, `avg2` copies the value of `avg1`, and is free to change its value without affecting the value of `avg1`. Reference types, on the other hand, share content by default. Changing one of the variables will change the underlying value that each reference shares.

```
let dateComponents1 = NSDateComponents()
dateComponents1.setValue(10, forComponent: .Day)
dateComponents1.day // => 10
var dateComponents2 = dateComponents1
dateComponents2.setValue(2, forComponent: .Day)
dateComponents1.day // => 2
dateComponents2.day // => 2
```

In this example, we use the reference type `NSDateComponents` to create `dateComponents1` and set the day calendar unit to 10. We then create another variable and assign our first value to it. Since both variables share their underlying data, modifying either variable changes both values.

Nested enumerations

The Foundation framework takes advantage of Swift 3's new nested enumeration feature. This feature allows the migrator to import related Objective-C enumerations into Swift under a common type. For example, the `NSDateFormatterStyle` and `NSDateFormatterBehavior` enumerations are imported as nested enumerations to the `DateFormatter` class in Swift. Let's see how we get to a nested enumeration in Swift 3, starting with an Objective-C enumeration.

In Objective-C:

```
typedef NS_ENUM(NSUInteger, NSDateFormatterStyle),
{
    NSDateFormatterNoStyle      = kCFDateFormatterNoStyle,
    NSDateFormatterShortStyle   = kCFDateFormatterShortStyle,
    NSDateFormatterMediumStyle  = kCFDateFormatterMediumStyle,
    NSDateFormatterLongStyle    = kCFDateFormatterLongStyle,
    NSDateFormatterFullStyle    = kCFDateFormatterFullStyle
};

typedef NS_ENUM(NSUInteger, NSDateFormatterBehavior){
    NSDateFormatterBehaviorDefault = 0,
    NSDateFormatterBehavior10_0    = 1_000,
    NSDateFormatterBehavior10_4    = 1_040,
};
```

In Swift 2.2-Better but not quite done:

```
enum NSDateFormatterStyle : UInt {
    case NoStyle
    case ShortStyle
    case MediumStyle
    case LongStyle
    case FullStyle
}

enum NSDateFormatterBehavior : UInt {
    case BehaviorDefault
    case Behavior10_0
    case Behavior10_4
}
```

In Swift 3:

```
DateFormatter {

    public enum Style : UInt {
        case none
        case short
        case medium
        case long
        case full
    }

    public enum Behavior : UInt {
        case `default`
        case behavior10_4
    }
}
```

Working with nested enumerations in Swift 3 is an improvement over Swift 2.2 because we no longer have to worry about a polluted global namespace of C-based enumerations.

Strongly typed string enumerations

The Foundation framework has a lot of string-based constants. For example, UIKit uses NSNotifications to publishing notifications for an iOS app's lifecycle.

```
NSString *const UIApplicationDidEnterBackgroundNotification
NSString *const UIApplicationWillEnterForegroundNotification        NSString
*const UIApplicationDidFinishLaunchingNotification;
```

New for Foundation, Objective-C now has the ability to use strongly typed string enumerations. This new feature allowed the Foundation team to update the enumerations in Objective-C. Our notifications listed earlier can now use the NSNotificationName type and convert our preceding constants to:

In Objective-C:

```
typedef NSString *NSNotificationName NS_EXTENSIBLE_STRING_ENUM;
NSNotificationName const UIApplicationDidEnterBackgroundNotification
NSNotificationName const UIApplicationWillEnterForegroundNotification
NSNotificationName const UIApplicationDidFinishLaunchingNotification;
```

In Swift, `NSNotificationName` types are imported as an extension on
`NSNotification.Name`.

```
extension NSNotification.Name {
public static let UIApplicationDidEnterBackground: NSNotification.Name
public static let UIApplicationWillEnterForeground: NSNotification.Name
public static let UIApplicationDidFinishLaunching: NSNotification.Name
}
```

Class properties

For historical reasons, the Foundation framework contains many cases where the state of a
property is closely associated with the type. Therefore, you will find lots of class properties
on Objective-C types. New for the Swift 3 release, we get a tweak to Objective-C that allows
us to use a new syntax for creating class properties. These class properties in Objective-C
will be imported into Swift as class properties as well.

In Objective-C (old way):

```
@interface NSCharacterSet
+ (NSCharacterSet *)controlCharacterSet;
+ (NSCharacterSet *)whitespaceCharacterSet;
+ (NSCharacterSet *)whitespaceAndNewlineCharacterSet;
@end
```

In Objective-C (new way):

```
@interface NSCharacterSet
@property(class, readonly, strong) controlCharacterSet;
@property(class, readonly, strong) whitespaceCharacterSet;
@property(class, readonly, strong) whitespaceAndNewlineCharacterSet;
@end
```

In Swift 2.2:

```
class NSCharacterSet{
 class func controlCharacters() -> NSCharacterSet
 class func whitespaces() -> NSCharacterSet
 class func whitespacesAndNewlines() -> NSCharacterSet
}
```

In Swift 3:

```
class NSCharacterSet{
  class var controlCharacters: CharacterSet { get }
  class var whitespaces: CharacterSet { get }
  class var whitespacesAndNewlines: CharacterSet { get }
}
```

Type safe access with value types

New with Swift 3, you can use Foundation value types to get compile time checks to eliminate many of the errors that couldn't be discovered until runtime when using reference-based Foundation types. Let's work through an example that demonstrates a runtime check in Swift 2.2.

In Swift 2.2:

```
if let filePath = NSBundle.mainBundle().pathForResource("testFile", ofType:
"txt"){
    let fileURL = NSURL.fileURLWithPath(filePath)
    let keys = [NSURLCreationDateKey, NSURLPathKey,
NSURLFileSizeKey,NSURLTagNamesKey]
    var values = try fileURL.resourceValuesForKeys(keys)
    if let creationDate = values[NSURLCreationDateKey]{
        print("creationDate: \(creationDate)")
    }
    values[NSURLTagNamesKey] = ["test", "sample", "playground"]
    values[NSURLCreationDateKey] = "now"    // à creates an error
    print(values[NSURLTagNamesKey])
    print(values[NSURLCreationDateKey])
    try fileURL.setResourceValues(values)
}
```

In our example, I created a reference to an existing file named `testFile.txt`. I would like to know some of the attributes of the file, which I can get by passing an array of strings to the `resourceValuesForKeys` method of my file reference. I can read the values using subscript notation and even update the values. Further, I can write the new values back to file with the `setResourceValues` method. The problem we experience is subtle and not shown until we execute this block of code. The `NSURLCreationDateKey` expects its value to be a valid `NSDate`.

However, I passed a string value. At runtime, our code block crashes with an error as we attempt to update our file with the new resource values. What we want is a way to check our constraints at compile time. Swift 3 now gives us a way to do this, and the Foundation framework has been updated to reflect this new feature. Let's update our example to reflect using type safe access to our file resources.

In Swift 3:

```
if let filePath = Bundle.main.path(forResource: "testFile",
ofType: "txt") {
    var fileURL = URL(fileURLWithPath: filePath)
    let keys: Set<URLResourceKey> = [.creationDateKey, .pathKey,
                                     .fileSizeKey, .tagNamesKey]
    let values = try fileURL.resourceValues(forKeys: keys)
    if let creationDate = values.creationDate{
        print("creationDate: \(creationDate)")
    }

    var newvalues = values
    newvalues.creationDate = "now"
    //error: cannot assign value of type 'String' to type 'Date?'
    //    newvalues.creationDate = "now"
    //                             ^~~~~
}
```

In our updated example, our resource types are now strongly typed values of type `URLResourceKey`. When we request the resources from our file, we are returned a struct that contains strongly typed properties. These two changes allow us to have type safe access and help us to catch issues at compile time. That's a pretty nice feature to have and the Foundation team agrees, which is evident by all of the APIs they updated to provide us better type constraints.

Measurements and units

With Swift 3's release, the Foundation team is releasing a new API to make handling measurements easier for developers. By allowing developers to create measurements from common built-in units (or create custom ones), convert between units and format them for display. We will cover each of the main areas of the Measurement API to get you ready to use them in your projects.

Measurement

A measurement is composed of a unit and a value. A unit is a class that contains a single property to hold a symbol. We will come back to units in a moment. For now, let's focus on what you can do with a measurement.

```
public struct Measurement<UnitType : Unit> : ReferenceConvertible,
Comparable, Equatable {

    public typealias ReferenceType = NSMeasurement

    /// The unit component of the `Measurement`.
    public let unit: UnitType

    /// The value component of the `Measurement`.
    public var value: Double

    /// Create a `Measurement` given a specified value and unit.
    public init(value: Double, unit: UnitType)
}

let initialAngle = Measurement(value: 30, unit: UnitAngle.degrees)
let maxAngle = Measurement(value: 90, unit: UnitAngle.degrees)
var currentAngle = initialAngle * 2.5   // 75.0 °
if currentAngle > maxAngle{
    print("Angle is greater than max supported angle")
}
```

With a measurement, we can define a value and its unit type, which can be used to convert to another type. We also gain validation that we aren't mixing measurement values that don't work together. It would not necessarily make sense to add a length unit to one that stores a volume. Without the measurement's API, you would have to write your own methods to ensure the proper constraints held true.

Unit and dimension

A *Unit* is a class that has symbol property. A `Dimension` is a subclass of `Unit` and is used to express categories of units. A `Dimension` contains a base unit and allows conversion between units via the `UnitConverter` type. `Dimension` types also contain singletons for many of the common units you will encounter when dealing with measurements.

```
class Unit : NSObject, NSCopying, NSSecureCoding {
    open var symbol: String { get }
    public init(symbol: String)
}
```

```
class Dimension : Unit, NSSecureCoding {
    @NSCopying open var converter: UnitConverter { get }
    public init(symbol: String, converter: UnitConverter)
    class func baseUnit() -> Self
}
```

The following table contains a listing of the `Dimension` subclasses that are available with Foundation.

Table 2, Dimension subclasses:

UnitAcceleration	UnitAngle	UnitArea
UnitConcentrationMass	UnitDispersion	UnitDuration
UnitElectricCharge	UnitElectricCurrent	UnitElectricPotentialDifference
UnitElectricResistance	UnitEnergy	UnitFrequency
UnitFuelEfficiency	UnitLength	UnitIlluminance
UnitMass	UnitPower	UnitPressure
UnitSpeed	UnitTemperature	UnitVolume

When using the built-in `Dimension` subclasses, you get basic conversion for free. For example, I created a `boxHeight` measurement with units of `UnitLength.feet` and a *smallBoxHeight* with units of `UnitLength.inches`. Next, I added the two measurements together and stored the value. The `totalHeight` variable stores the combined value using `UnitLength` base value of meters.

```
let boxHeight = Measurement(value: 3.2, unit: UnitLength.feet)
let smallBoxHeight = Measurement(value: 20, unit: UnitLength.inches)
let totalHeight = boxHeight + smallBoxHeight
print(totalHeight) // 1.48336 m
```

We can also use our comparison operations like ==, >, < because our measurements convert to the base unit before doing the conversions.

```
if boxHeight > smallBoxHeight{
    print("boxHeight is still larger")
}
```

Custom units

There are going to be times when you need a unit type that doesn't conform to one of the pre-built `Dimension` subclasses. To make your own units, you will need to create a unit type on an existing `Dimension`, supplying a symbol and unit converter function.

```
let burgerSymbol = "\u{1F354}" //
let burgers = UnitLength(symbol: burgerSymbol , converter:
UnitConverterLinear(coefficient: 2))
```

You can add new units to any of the `Dimension` subclasses. Our preceding example creates a new `burgers` unit on `UnitLength`. If you need more of a time-based unit, you could create a unit on `UnitDuration`.

```
let gittieSecond = UnitDuration(symbol: "gs", converter:
UnitConverterLinear(coefficient: 0.5))
```

By providing a converter function, you ensure that your unit can be converted between its unit and the base unit on the `Dimension` with which it is associated.

Custom Dimension types

Now that we know how to create our new units for the `Dimension` subclasses, the questions that begs to be asked is whether you can create custom `Dimension` types. As you might have already guessed, creating a new `Dimension` subclass is also possible and straightforward.

```
public class ToddlerMovement: Dimension{
    static let tummyCrawl = ToddlerMovement(symbol: "crawls", converter:
UnitConverterLinear(coefficient: 0.25))
    static let allFours = ToddlerMovement(symbol: "allfours", converter:
UnitConverterLinear(coefficient: 2.0))
    static let shakySteps = ToddlerMovement(symbol: "shaky_steps",
converter: UnitConverterLinear(coefficient: 1))
}

let playPenDistance = Measurement(value: 4, unit:
ToddleMovement.tummyCrawl)
let kitchenFloorDistance = Measurement(value: 20, unit:
ToddleMovement.shakySteps)
let almostThereDistance = Measurement(value: 10, unit:
ToddleMovement.allFours)

print(playPinDistance) // 4.0 crawls
```

```
print(kitchenFloorDistance) // 20.0 shaky_steps
print(almostThereDistance)  // 10.0 allfours
```

Convert functions

In each of the prior `Measurement` examples, we used the `UnitConverterLinear` function as our converter function. As mentioned earlier, you need to include a converter function any time you add a new unit to a `Dimension`. The converter method is used to convert to and from the `Dimension` base unit value. The `UnitConverterLinear` converter allows you to make conversions between units when the relation is linear (for example, $y = mx + b$). This class has two initializers:

1. One to provide just the slope (coefficient or m in our line equation) when there is no offset.
2. The other to allow you to provide both a slope and offset (b).

```
class UnitConverterLinear : UnitConverter {
    var coefficient: Double { get }
    var constant: Double { get }
    init(coefficient: Double)
    init(coefficient: Double, constant: Double)
}
```

Linear Conversion:

```
baseUnit = value * coefficient + constant
value = (baseUnit - constant) / coefficient
```

The `UnitConverterLinear` converter is really useful and will allow you to cover many conversions by just providing the ratio between two unit values. However, this converter won't fit every relationship between two units. Therefore, you can also subclass `UnitConverter` and create a conversion formula that meets your use case when the need arises.

```
class UnitConverter : NSObject {
    open func baseUnitValue(fromValue value: Double) -> Double
    open func value(fromBaseUnitValue baseUnitValue: Double) -> Double
}
```

If you choose to create your own custom unit converter, you are will need to override the `baseUnitValue(fromValue value: Double)` and `value(fromBaseUnitValue baseUnitValue: Double)` methods. These two methods are used internally to perform conversions for you.

Formatting measurements

Dealing with formatting is tough, and you don't have to look any further than the
NSDateFormatter to see how complicated things could be when working with dates.
Fortunately, the Foundation team added a new measurements formatter to do all of the
heavy lifting for us. MeasurementFormatter will handle formatting our Measurements
and Unit types, while taking into account the user's locale.

```
class MeasurementFormatter : Formatter, NSSecureCoding {
    var unitOptions: MeasurementFormatter.UnitOptions
    var unitStyle: Formatter.UnitStyle
    @NSCopying var locale: Locale!
    @NSCopying var numberFormatter: NumberFormatter!
    func string(from measurement: Measurement<Unit>) -> String
    func string(from unit: Unit) -> String
}
```

The UnitOptions property on MeasurementFormatter is a special property that we need
to take a moment to discuss. The UnitOptions property is a struct on the
MeasurementFormatter and instructs our formatter to use the preferred unit of the user's
locale by default.

```
extension MeasurementFormatter {
    public struct UnitOptions : OptionSet {
    public init(rawValue: UInt)
    public static var providedUnit:
                            MeasurementFormatter.UnitOptions { get }
    public static var naturalScale:
                            MeasurementFormatter.UnitOptions { get }
    public static var temperatureWithoutUnit:
                            MeasurementFormatter.UnitOptions { get }
    }
}
```

In our example here, we create a custom unit (*gittieSecond*) and a measurement using
this unit. We then create a MeasurementFormatter and call the string method, passing
our measurement, to get a formatted measurement using the Dimension base unit. Even
though our custom unit has a gs symbol, the formatter converts and displays our
measurement using seconds.

```
let formatter = MeasurementFormatter()
let gittieSecond = UnitDuration(symbol: "gs", converter:
UnitConverterLinear(coefficient: 0.5))
let getterThere = Measurement(value: 5, unit: gittieSecond) // 5.0 gs
let formattedGS = formmatter.string(from: getterThere)
print(formattedGS) // 2.5 sec
```

To change the output of the formatter from using the base unit to instead use our gittieSecond unit, we need to modify the UnitOptions property on the formatter. In my locale, the preferred unit for UnitDuration is seconds. By changing the UnitOptions use reference providedUnit, we ensure that our formatter will use the same unit as the getterThere measurement passed to the formatter.

```
formatter.unitOptions = .providedUnit
formatter.string(from: getterThere) // 5 gs
```

Summary

In this chapter, we covered changes to the Foundation framework. We started with a discussion on mutability and new value types in Foundation. You learned that both value and reference types have their place in our code. Next, we covered nested enumerations and strongly typed string enumerations. We explored class properties and the type-safe access benefits of value types. Finally, we spent a great deal of time discussing the new Measurements API introduced this year in Foundation. In the next chapter, we will cover testing and debugging. Swift 3 introduces several changes in testing and debugging that should help improve the quality of the code you write.

9
Improving Your Code with Xcode Server and LLDB Debugging

One of the biggest skills you can learn to improve in your code is by learning how to test it. Adding unit tests to your code with the `XCTest` Testing framework will help you improve the quality of your code and will provide a secondary benefit of documenting how your code works. As you move from solo developer projects to multi-member teams, it becomes harder to maintain tests that are written in isolation. Automated testing, added to a continuous integration pipeline on a server, helps to address these pain points in the same way that source repositories help to manage code over larger projects.

In the first part of this chapter, we will cover Xcode Server's capabilities as a continuous integration server and how automated testing can be included to improve your testing workflow. In the second half, we will describe how to use LLDB for debugging your code on Linux.

Continuous integration overview with Xcode server

Using server-based testing has several benefits that could justify the time investment for your team. If you're on the fence about whether going this route works for your team, make sure to consider the following in your evaluations:

1. Moving your builds and unit tests to a server frees your local box to keep working on features and debugging, while your builds and test suites run remotely.
2. Build triggers can run your tests on code check-ins and alert your team when things change expectantly due to tests failing.
3. Tests on your server are consistent and run the same way each time; meaning that individual developer environment and project tweaks won't affect test runs.
4. You can schedule full test suites to run at your convenience and short running tests to execute on every code check-in as an example.
5. You can have your tests executed against multiple development environments and hardware. For example, you could have your test run on multiple iPad models and OS versions along with several iPhones with ease using a server environment. This would be a time-consuming task to do manually.

A continuous integration workflow is a process that starts with developing locally on a development machine and then checking your code into a repository. Next, you migrate your project to Xcode server for processing. In order for Xcode Server to process your code, you have to provide it with some instructions in the form of *bots*. On your development box, you create *bots* with your processing rules that run on Xcode Server. The execution of a *bot* is called an *integration*, which can be run manually or according to a schedule. Once an *integration* finishes, the activity is reported back to your development Mac.

Bot features

Without *bots*, you can't do anything useful with Xcode Server. *Bots* build your code and run your tests, using a supplied Xcode project scheme. A well-crafted *bot* can control when it runs and how it communicates its activity to you and your team. For instance, you could have the *bot* run when a new commit has occurred and have it e-mail the *integration* status (for example, success or failure) to you and/or your development team. You can also add pre and post *integration* triggers that can execute scripts to communicate with web services or to run additional performance tests based on initial *integration* outputs.

Monitoring and managing bots

Once you have created your *bots*, you can manage and monitor them in Xcode Server. Xcode Server can be configured to push *bot* statuses to your development Mac, provide a web hook to view activity in a browser or third-party app (for example, Slack/HipChat), or send you an e-mail report. On your development Mac, you can see very detailed reports using the report navigator in Xcode.

Configuring Xcode server

To use Xcode server, you have to download and install macOS Server (formerly known as OS X Server) from the App Store on a Mac.

 Installing is straightforward, and you can find detailed instructions at
`https://developer.apple.com/library/prerelease/content/documenta`
`tion/IDEs/Conceptual/xcode_guide-`
`continuous_integration/adopt_continuous_integration.html -`
`//apple_ref/doc/uid/TP40013292-CH3-SW1.`

Adding repositories for the Xcode server

The Xcode Server needs a code repository to do work and is compatible with either Git or Subversion. Any *bots* that you create will need access to a repository. A bot will try to connect to a repository via SSH or HTTPS. Apple does a really good job of describing your repository setup options.

 You can refer to the following section of their setup guide for step-by-step instructions on how to configure your repos to give access to Xcode Server and your *bot*:
`https://developer.apple.com/library/prerelease/content/documenta`
`tion/IDEs/Conceptual/xcode_guide-`
`continuous_integration/PublishYourCodetoaSourceRepository.html -`
`//apple_ref/doc/uid/TP40013292-CH8-SW1.`

Configuring bots

A *bot* is a process, run by the Xcode Server to build and test code from a source repository. Each time you run an instance of your bot, you are performing what's known as *integration*. You create a *bot* and add an associated scheme to the *bot* that references your development box. The *bot* creation wizard walks you through options for choosing the scheme to use, setting the frequency to run, and providing any shell scripts to run before or after an *integration*.

 You can read more about how to setup a bot at
`https://developer.apple.com/library/tvos/documentation/IDEs/Conc`
`eptual/xcode_guide-continuous_integration/ConfigureBots.html` —
`//apple_ref/doc/uid/TP40013292-CH9-SW1.`

Last year, Xcode Server introduced a new feature that allows us to add custom environment variables that our *bots* can access. This year Xcode Server allows us to add pre and post scripts that will run on each *integration*. This feature could allow you to pre-load your environment with external files or data for unit testing before your *bot* builds and executes tests. Another example might be to have a post *integration* script communicate with a Rest API to send the success or failure status.

Managing and monitoring your integration runs

You can access detailed reports on *integration* runs for each *bot* in Xcode's Report Navigator (**View** | **Navigators** | **Show Report Navigator**). This view also gives you the ability to create additional *bots* or edit existing ones. Selecting any of the *bots* listed in the sidebar gives you a summary report of the integration results.

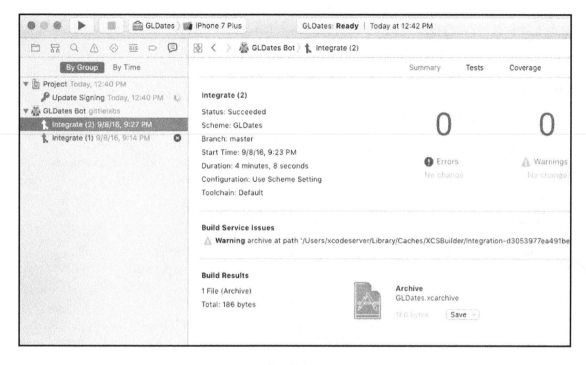

Report Navigator

Debugging with LLDB

LLDB is the debugger that powers Xcode. In Xcode's debug console, you can find a console window that gives you access to an *LLDB* prompt. On Linux or from the command line, you can access *LLDB* from the Swift *REPL*. Let's explore how we can use *LLDB* to debug our programs using some of the commands of which you may or may not already be aware.

You can read more about debugging with LLDB in the LLDB Debugging Guide:
`https://developer.apple.com/library/prerelease/content/documenta`
`tion/General/Conceptual/lldb-guide/chapters/Introduction.html` —
`//apple_ref/doc/uid/TP40016717-CH1-DontLinkElementID_42.`

LLDB command syntax

Interacting with *LLDB* is as easy as entering a command into the prompt. The command structure contains zero or more subcommands followed by zero or more options or arguments.

```
<command> [<subcommand>...] [--<option> [<option-value>]]... [argument]...
```

Subcommands and arguments are space-delimited tokens; while options are space delimited, but use double dashes (and sometimes single dash) as a prefix. An example *LLDB* command would be to set a breakpoint on a function. In the following example, we would set a breakpoint for the speakToMe() function:

```
(lldb) breakpoint set -n speakToMe
```

You can always get help by typing help at the *LLDB* prompt. Typing help without arguments will list all of the commands available with short descriptions:

```
(lldb) help
```

You can get help on a specific command by typing help along with the command name or the command name and subcommand name for even more specialized results.

```
(lldb) help breakpoint
(lldb) help breakpoint set
```

Managing breakpoints

Breakpoints are the main way to interrupt your running program for inspection at specific points. We can create, modify, delete, or list breakpoints through *LLDB*.

Creating a breakpoint

We use the breakpoint set command to create a breakpoint:

```
4> func sayHello(){
  5.     print("Hi")
  6. }
  7> sayHello()
Hi
  8> :breakpoint set --name sayHello
Breakpoint 1: where = $__lldb_expr5`__lldb_expr_4.sayHello () -> () + 4 at
```

```
repl.swift:5, address = 0x00000001005c6064
```

Listing breakpoints

We use the `breakpoint list` command to list the names and locations of breakpoints in a program:

```
(lldb) breakpoint list
Current breakpoints:
1: name = 'sayHello', locations = 1, resolved = 1, hit count = 1
   1.1: where = $__lldb_expr5`__lldb_expr_4.sayHello () -> () + 4 at
repl.swift:5, address = 0x00000001005c6064, resolved, hit count = 1
```

Modifying a breakpoint

Another interesting thing you can do with breakpoints is to add conditions on activation. Using the `breakpoint modify` command, you can use any of the following options to change the target breakpoint's behavior.

```
-D ( --dummy-breakpoints ) : Sets Dummy breakpoints

-T <thread-name> ( --thread-name <thread-name> ) The breakpoint stops only
for the thread whose thread name matches this argument.

-c <expr> ( --condition <expr> ) The breakpoint stops only if this
condition expression evaluates to true.

-d ( --disable ) Disable the breakpoint.
-e ( --enable )Enable the breakpoint.
-i <count> ( --ignore-count <count> ) Set the number of times this
breakpoint is skipped before stopping.
-o <boolean> ( --one-shot <boolean> ) The breakpoint is deleted the first
time it stop causes a stop.
-q <queue-name> ( --queue-name <queue-name> ) The breakpoint stops only for
threads in the queue whose name is given by this argument.
-t <thread-id> ( --thread-id <thread-id> ) The breakpoint stops only for
the thread whose TID matches this argument.
-x <thread-index> ( --thread-index <thread-index> ) The breakpoint stops
only for the thread whose index matches this argument.
```

Enabling and disabling a breakpoint

You can enable and disable a breakpoint using either the breakpoint ID or the location. You pass the ID to the `enable` or `disable` subcommands:

```
(lldb) breakpoint enable 1.1
1 breakpoint enabled.

(lldb) breakpoint disable 1.1
1 breakpoint disabled.
```

Deleting a breakpoint

When you no longer need your breakpoint, you can simply remove it using the delete subcommand with the breakpoint ID or location:

```
(lldb) breakpoint delete 1.1
```

Command aliases

Command aliases allow you to create a shorter syntax for commands that you use often. You can also provide help text to accompany your alias. You can see additional details on how to manage a command alias by typing `help command`.

```
(lldb) help command
        Commands for managing custom LLDB commands.

Syntax: command <subcommand> [<subcommand-options>]

The following subcommands are supported:

      alias   -- Define a custom command in terms of an existing command.  Expects 'raw' input (see 'help raw-input'.)
      delete  -- Delete one or more custom commands defined by 'command regex'.
      history -- Dump the history of commands in this session.
      regex   -- Define a custom command in terms of existing commands by matching regular expressions.
      script  -- Commands for managing custom commands implemented by interpreter scripts.
      source  -- Read and execute LLDB commands from the file <filename>.
      unalias -- Delete one or more custom commands defined by 'command alias'.

For more help on any particular subcommand, type 'help <command> <subcommand>'.
```

In the following example, we create a command alias to execute a command we pass to our alias using the Unix shell:

```
(lldb) command alias -h "Run a command in the Unix shell" -- shell platform shell
(lldb) help shell
     Run a command in the Unix shell  Expects 'raw' input (see 'help raw-input'.)

Syntax: shell <cmd-options>

Command Options Usage:
  shell [-t <value>]

     -t <value> ( --timeout <value> )
         Seconds to wait for the remote host to finish running the command.

     Important Note: Because this command takes 'raw' input, if you use any command options you must use ' -- ' between the end of
     the command options and the beginning of the raw input.

'shell' is an abbreviation for 'platform shell'
(lldb) shell whoami
vagrant
(lldb)
```

Summary

In this chapter, we covered the basics of a continuous integration workflow using Xcode Server. You learned what a bot is and how they are used to build and test your code on Xcode Server. With the addition of Swift on Linux, we needed to explore other options outside Xcode for testing code. LLDB is extremely powerful and even has customization options for your debugging sessions. In our next and final chapter, we will discuss writing Swift on a Linux server.

10
Exploring Swift on the Server

Unless you're making a really basic app, chances are that you will need some form of server backend to make your app really useful. Swift running on Linux is a big deal, especially with Linux's popularity for hosting and running servers. Swift 3 opens up possibilities for developers to create server-side applications using the same Swift that they use to create applications on iOS, macOS, tvOS, and watchOS. By the end of this chapter, you will have a server-side app written completely in Swift that can run seamlessly on a Linux box.

IBM Swift Package catalog

In `Chapter 2`, *Discovering New Territories – Linux at Last!* we covered installing Swift toolchains and configuring environments for Linux. We wrote our first program in Swift and leveraged the Swift Package Manager to manage our dependencies. With the basics out of the way, I want to mention IBM's Swift Package Catalog.

The IBM Swift Package Catalog is a site that hosts links to Swift libraries and modules that you can use with the Swift Package Manager. IBM wants it to be a community resource for developers to find and share code for their projects. You can find the site listed at the following link `https://developer.ibm.com/swift/the-ibm-swift-package-catalog`. You should definitely keep this link handy, as it will be a site that you will use often. You can explore projects based on rank, popularity, or keywords.

Introducing our server project

Let's go out with a bang! For this last chapter, we are going to create a small project to test developing a server app in Swift. We will use the IBM Swift Package Catalog to find a web server framework. I really like using Slack for team communication. If you haven't tried it, you should consider evaluating whether it could be a good tool for your team. One of the powerful features of Slack is the array of integration options you have to customize the experience for your team. Slack has opened many of its APIs to developers for customization and integration. Slack even provides an App Store for users to add third-party apps that their teams can use together. The catch, if there is one, is that your third-party app or integration has to be hosted on an outside server. We are going to create a Slack integration that you can later modify into a full Slack app of your own. Our Slack integration will be written entirely in Swift, and it could be hosted on a Linux virtual machine in the cloud with a provider such as Heroku, Digital Ocean, or Amazon Web Services.

 You can download the code for this project from `http://www.packtpub.c om/support` .

Project description and dependencies

Our project needs a web server framework to work properly. We could write one from scratch, or we could see what third-party frameworks are available. Using the IBM Swift Package Catalog, I found several web application frameworks that are highly rated and are both actively developed and popular with developers. IBM's Kitura, Perfect by PerfectlySoft, and Vapor by Vapor are all viable candidates from which to choose. Each of these projects will feel familiar to you if you have ever dabbled with Node.js and Express, or with Ruby on Rails. While any of these frameworks would work for our project, I selected the Vapor project for our app because it was at the top of the list in the "essential" category at the time I was writing this chapter.

According to Vapor, their project is the most used web framework written for Swift. You can learn more about Vapor, including the Swift version it supports and links to the documentation, at `https://swiftpkgs.ng.bluemix.net/package/vapor/vapor`.

Now that we have covered the libraries and frameworks that we will use, let me give you a description of the server application that we will be building together. Slack gives developers the option to create custom integrations for their own team or to make Slack apps that would be available to any team. We are going to create a custom integration for a single team. However, you could easily convert our customization into a full app for any team to discover.

We are going to build a storefront web application to sell widgets. As a user purchases a widget from us, we will process the order and send the order to our order-tracking channel in Slack. In the interest of keeping this application simple, we are going to take some shortcuts.

Setting up our environment and project

Since you learned how to install Swift in Chapter 2, *Discovering New Territories – Linux at Last!* we will skip over that step and move on to installing the Vapor framework. We are going to add Vapor's command line toolkit to gain access to shortcut commands and assistance for common tasks.

 You can find detailed links to documentation and examples on how to use Vapor at https://vapor.github.io/documentation/.

Here's how you do it:

To install the toolkit, run the following command in a terminal:

```
curl -sL toolbox.vapor.sh | bash
```

You can verify that the command worked by running:

```
vapor -help
```

Next, let's create a new Vapor project and name it storefront:

```
vapor new storefront
```

Our newly created project will have the following file structure:

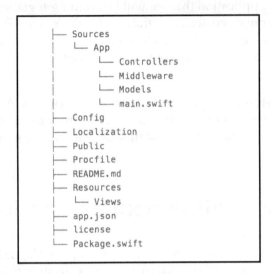

```
├── Sources
│    └── App
│         └── Controllers
│         └── Middleware
│         └── Models
│         └── main.swift
├── Config
├── Localization
├── Public
├── Procfile
├── README.md
├── Resources
│    └── Views
├── app.json
├── license
└── Package.swift
```

The file structure should be familiar to you, as it follows the structure required for the Swift Package Manager to work. Under the cover, vapor creates a new project with *swift package init–type executable*. The Vapor script also adds the vapor framework as a dependency in `Package.swift`. Our `main.swift` is our entry point, since we created an executable program.

I'm going to develop my code on a Mac and then deploy it to a Linux VM in the cloud. For me, the benefit is that I can use Xcode and it's debugging tools for my local development. In fact, the Vapor framework supports this concept by offering a command in their toolkit to generate an Xcode project for development. Let's create an Xcode project that we can use for development of our *storefront* app:

```
vapor xcode
```

When Vapor creates a companion Xcode project, it first checks to see if you are missing any dependencies specified in the Package.swift file. Vapor will download any missing dependencies for you, prior to creating the Xcode Project. In addition, Vapor will create a scheme to use for running your app in Xcode. Finally, Vapor will show you which toolchain the Xcode project expects to be linked against:

```
No Packages folder, fetch may take a while...
Fetching Dependencies [Done]
Generating Xcode Project [Done]
Select the `App` scheme to run.
```

```
Make sure Xcode > Toolchains > 3.0-GM-CANDIDATE is selected.
Open Xcode project?
y/n>nz
```

Whenever you create new dependencies for your project, you have to rebuild the project so that the Swift Package Manager can download your new dependency before attempting to compile your code:

vapor clean or vapor build --clean

Let's take a quick look at `Package.swift` to see what the Vapor create command generated for us. We can configure the name of the app with something that better suits our project. The current default name is `VaporApp`, but we could change this to `Storefront`. You should also notice that the vapor framework is added for us as a dependency.

```
import PackageDescription

let package = Package(
    name: "VaporApp",
    dependencies: [
        .Package(url: "https://github.com/vapor/vapor.git", majorVersion:
0, minor: 18)
],
    exclude: [
        "Config",
        "Database",
        "Localization",
        "Public",
        "Resources",
        "Tests",
    ]
)
```

When you use the Vapor CLI to create a new project, Vapor adds example code with documentation to project. Open `main.swift` and glance over the included routes and comments. Delete everything in this file, and we will be build our app from scratch.

The Vapor framework

In Vapor terminology, a Droplet is a service container that acts as a gateway to Vapor's service offerings. Use a Droplet to register routes and add middleware to start your server. To get things started, we need to import Vapor and create an instance of a Droplet.

```
import Vapor

let drop = Droplet()
```

We can also customize the behavior of our Droplet instance via properties. You can read more about options in Vapor's documentation.

Routing

Now that we have a Droplet instance, we need to talk about routing. Routing is an essential function for every web framework. When an incoming request is received, we need to have a way to appropriately filter and handle each request. Vapor gives you multiple options for addressing your routing concerns. We are going to create two routes for our application: one to serve our shop page, and the other to respond to *post* requests when a user purchases an item on our page.

A basic route in Vapor is composed of a method, path, and closure. Two of our routes fall into this category. Vapor routing supports the standard RESTful HTTP methods (get, post, put, patch, delete, and options). We register routes by calling the corresponding method on our Droplet instance, passing in our route path and returning a closure we define.

```
drop.get("/") { request in
    return try drop.view.make("shop.html")
}

drop.post("purchase") { request in

// more stuff happening here but omitted

var response = try Response(status: .ok, json: json)
    return response
}
```

Our first route handles all *get* requests for the root directory of our website. When this route is requested, we return the `shop.html` view. Our second route handles *post* requests for the `/purchase` route. Once we finish carrying out work, we return a response to the requester with a status and JSON payload.

Vapor also supports nested routes and parameters. Creating a nested route is as easy as replacing the forward slashes in the URL with commas when registering your route.

```
// Nested route
drop.get("products", "vehicles", "trucks") { request in
    return "You requested /products/vehicles/trucks"
}
```

Vapor handles parameters by making them type safe. Many web frameworks default to using strings for route parameters and types, which can be error prone. Using Swift's closures allows for a safer way to access route parameters. In the following example, we define the route to accept an *Int* parameter. Our route matches *artboard/:id* where our *:id* parameter must be an Integer value.

```
// Type Safe parameters
drop.get("artboard", Int.self) { request, productId in
    return "You requested Artboard #\(productId)"
}
```

We could have also written this without using route parameters and then access our parameters on the request object.

```
drop.get("artboard", ":id") { request in
    guard let productId = request.parameters["id"]?.int else {
        throw Abort.badRequest
    }
    return "You requested Artboard #\(productId)"
}
```

Creating views

When you want to send HTML from your application, you create views. You can create a view from an HTML document or you can build your views using renderers like Mustache. By default, views are stored in the *Resources/Views* directory. Going back to the first route registered for our root directory, we used a view to return an HTML document (shop.html). You create an instance of a view by calling the view.make method on your Droplet instance.

```
drop.get("/") { request in
    return try drop.view.make("shop.html")
}
```

More complex documents, such as mustache templates, need more information to process and create a view. This additional information is passed to the *view.make* method as the second argument.

```
drop.get("shop_template") { request in
    return try drop.view.make("shop.template", [
        "countdown": "2 days left",
        "shopper_count": "1,000"
        ])
}
```

Public resources

For the most part, we want all of our server code and files protected from snooping eyes and web crawlers. Vapor handles that for us. When we need to provide resources that are reachable from our views, we use the `Public` folder created at the root of our application. We will store our images, scripts, and styles nested under the `Public` folder.

Defining our shop view

When we serve the root level document on our application, we return a `shop.html` view. Our simple page displays a welcome message and details of three products.

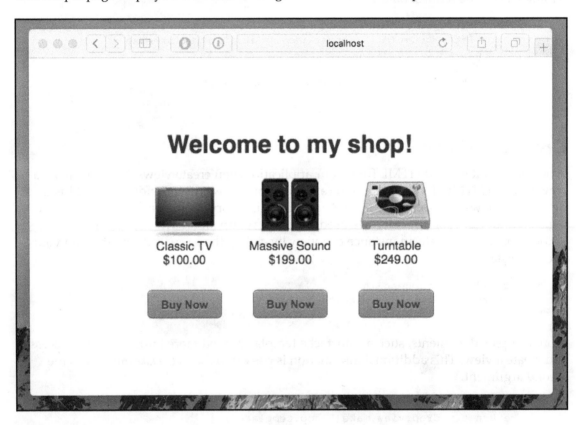

When a user clicks the buy now button, we execute a jQuery Ajax post command to communicate with our server. We send the product ID of the product we want to purchase to our `"/purchase"` route.

On the server, when we receive a request that matches this route, we extract the product ID and search for a matching product in our local store. Of course, in a production app, we would use a database to house our products and even populate our store listings. In situations where we can't find a valid product ID on our request object or where we can't find a matching product for a supplied product ID, we throw an error that is sent back to the client.

Finally, we create a JSON payload that contains some of our product details and return it to the client with a successful status code.

```
drop.post("purchase") { request in
    drop.log.info("purchase request made")
    guard let product_id = request.data["product_id"]?.int else {
        throw Abort.badRequest
    }
    guard let product = products.filter({ (prod) -> Bool in
        return prod.id == product_id
    }).first else{
        throw Abort.badRequest
    }

    let json = try JSON(node: [
        "Product" : "\(product.name)",
        "price" : "\(product.price)",
        ])

// more work happening and omitted

    var response = try Response(status: .ok, json: json)
    return response
}
```

When our client receives the post response, we display an alert dialog that thanks the user for their purchase. We also display the returned JSON data in a console.

Slack integration

Now that we covered the basics of our web app, let's make it a bit more interesting by integrating with Slack. Using Slack's APIs, we can extend Slack to make our workflow better. In our case, we want to notify our operations team of new orders so that they can immediately start processing them. We are going to take advantage of incoming webhooks to send messages into Slack from our Swift server. While this webhook will only be for our team, you can read the documentation `https://api.slack.com/` and easily convert our custom integration into a Slack app that any team could incorporate into their workflows.

Making a custom integration

Since our custom integration will only work with a single Slack team, you will need to create an account and team on Slack if you don't already have one. Once you do that, you can navigate to the build section of the Slack app directory located at :

1. Click on the **Make a Custom Integration** button.

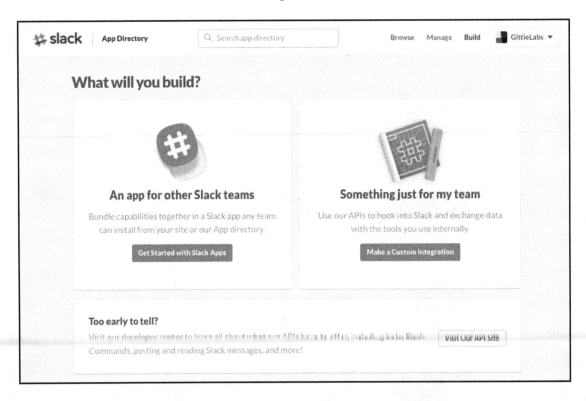

2. Select the **Incoming WebHooks** link next.

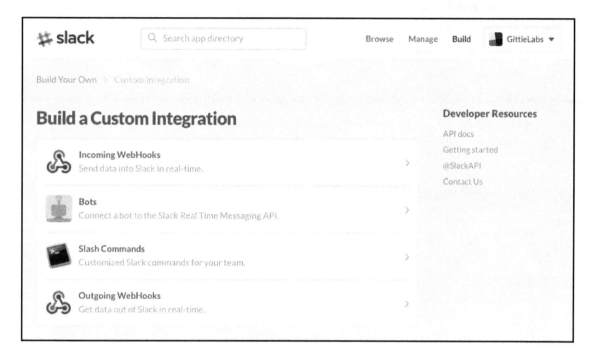

Choose a channel to post your messages to or create a new channel. I chose to send my messages to my orders channel. After picking your channel, press the "**Add Incoming WebHooks integration**" button.

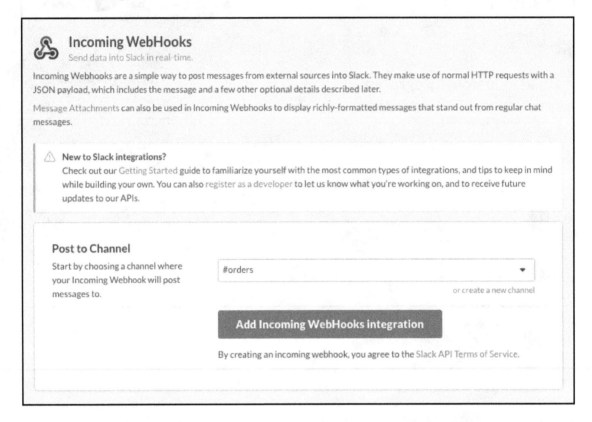

On this view, you can see instructions for setting things up as well as the fields you can customize for your use case. You can provide an optional descriptive label for this integration along with a user name. The default name is `incoming-webhook`, but I changed mine to `OrderUp`. I also added an emoji to serve as my icon for the messages I add to this channel. Once you have previewed your settings, you just need to click on the **Save Settings** button to make your changes go live.

Updating our server to post to Slack

Before we close this view, we need to copy the Webhook URL to use from our external service. You can click on the **Copy URL** button, and it will be added to your clipboard. Let's head back to Swift and open `main.swift`. Update your purchase route to create a JSON payload for Slack to send our post request to Slack's servers:

```
drop.post("purchase") { request in
  // omitted code above

    let slack_payload = try JSON(node: [ "attachments":
        try JSON(node: [
            try JSON(node: [
                "fallback": "New purchase Request",
                "pretext": "New purchase Request",
                "color": "#D00000",
                "fields": try JSON(node: [
                    try JSON(node: [
                        "title" : "Product: \(product.name)",
                        "value" : "Price: \(product.price)",
                        "short" : "false"
                        ])
                    ])
                ])
            ])
        ])
    _ = try drop.client.post("https://hooks.slack.com/services/<your hook
id>", headers: [:], query: [:], body: slack_payload)

    var response = try Response(status: .ok, json: json)
    return response
}
```

Our formatted message payload sends a general message, which will show up in your Slack notifications on desktop and mobile (`"New purchase Request"`). We also use the attachment syntax to provide details on the product order. We pass the product name and price.

Now, when you make a purchase on the website, you will also get a real-time message sent to the orders channel in Slack for your team.

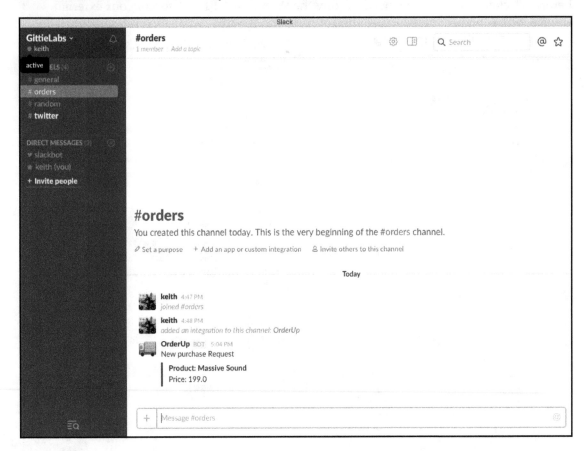

Summary

In this chapter, we explored Swift on the server. We developed a web application that runs entirely in Swift. Our application also communicates with Slack to post messages. We used the Vapor web framework to create a Swift web server, and you learned how to call Slack webhooks from Swift. While our example was fairly simple, it is easy to see how we could expand it to a larger and more complex application leveraging the power of Swift.

This brings us to the end of the book. We've covered a lot of material and learned the new features of Swift 3. We discussed Apple's motivation and objectives for the evolution of Swift. I have shown you where to find documentation on the language and how to get involved with the future direction of Swift. We explored Swift on Linux and some of the possibilities this creates for server-side Swift applications. Swift 3 adds new language features that improve many of the libraries that you will use everyday in your coding projects.

It's my hope that this book will prove to be a reference for you as dive into developing for Swift 3. While we have examined many of the features of the language, it isn't feasible to cover every single change to the language. While this book provides a good base for understanding the changes for Swift 3, you will need to apply what you've learned in your code. In addition, you should refer to Apple's documentation, and the Swift community to stay on top of the latest developments to the language. The best developers never rely on their current knowledge. They actively seek to learn more and more. If you want to master Swift 3, you will have to use all of the resources at your disposal to build on the base we created together. I know you can do it, and I wish you the best of luck in your journey.

Index

www.ingramcontent.com/pod-product-compliance
Lightning Source LLC
Chambersburg PA
CBHW060149060326
40690CB00018B/4044